SWANMORE
ON THE HOME FRONT
IN WORLD WAR II

Recollections and pictures
of a Hampshire village
in wartime

Edited by
Keith Harrington

Harringtons Heritage

Published by Harringtons Heritage
9 Glendale
Swanmore
Southampton SO32 2QY

First Edition 2006

ISBN-0-9554530-0-3   978-0-9554530-0-7

Sponsored by Home Front Recall
Supported by

Printed by Meon Valley Printers
Church Road, Swanmore, Southampton SO32 2PU
www.mvp.uk.com

To my grandchildren Chloe, Rebecca, James and Emily.
Thank you for the treasured moments
we have been able to spend together.

Photos (Front Cover)

Top Centre
The Defence Medal was awarded to many of those serving on the
Home Front e.g. The Home Guard, Womens Land Army, Voluntary
Aid Detachments (V.A.D.), Air Raid Protection (A.R.P.) units etc

Top Left
Jean Edney (V.A.D.) (Left), Joyce Edney (V.A.D.) (Right)
Vera Conduct (née Plenty) (Womens Land Army) (Centre)
(worked at Hill Cross Allotments 1942 - 46)

Top Right
Bucketts Farm Bomb Disposal Team

Bottom
Home Guard Standing Down Parade 1944 Sgt. Ron Crook holding Pennant

Contents

Foreword

Although the theme of this book is devoted to activity in Swanmore on the 'Home Front' during World War II (1939-1945), I have included other material, mainly photographic, that expands the period covered from circa 1930 to 1950. My reason for doing this is that many of those depicted or referred to would have reached adulthood during the hostilities and gone on to play their parts both at home and abroad in the battle for freedom.

With the help of many who were in Swanmore during the war, I have tried to get as complete and accurate a picture as possible, but errors will have crept in, for which I apologise. If you can point out some of these errors (or provide missing information), I would be very pleased to hear from you.

In producing this book I hope to be able to capture for posterity the fortitude and strength of character shown by all those involved, but I realise there are many people who played a very active part in the village's life at that time who, through the demands of space, I have not been able to mention. I am proud to have been able to call Swanmore 'home' for more than 30 years and trust that this book will bring pleasure to those who delve into its contents, particularly the members of the long-established village families without whose help and patience publication would have remained only a distant dream.

Keith Harrington

Acknowledgements

I would like to thank all contributors to the book: those who wrote articles and many others who have provided information, answered questions and reviewed drafts.
Some additional information has been extracted, with permission, from books included in the Bibliography at the end of this book, and some from web sites.

Illustrations are by courtesy of the following:

The Imperial War Museum
Hampshire Record Office
Swanmore Primary School   (Painting of School)
Stephenson Locomotive Soc. Collection   (Train at Droxford)
Ann Blackman (née Richards)   (Rising Sun)
Brian Conduct   (Womens Land Army)
Emily Elliott (née Wearne)   (Scouts)
Vic Feltham   (H.M.S. Duncton)
Doris Fitall (née Willoughby)   (Methodist Church)
Ron French   (Holywell/Dieppe Raid)
Kathleen Hartley (née Watson)   (Hillgrove Farm)
Terry Harvey   (Fire Brigade)
Gwen Hobbs (née Kirby)   (Bricklayers Arms/Miscellaneous)
Mary Junor
and Celia McGarry (née Junor)   (The Junor Family)
Alma Parsons (née Edney)   (Miscellaneous)
Vi Searle (née Wilkinson)   (Cortursel)
Vera Tribbeck   (Miscellaneous)
Kenneth Ward   (Droxford)
John Watson (of Shapeton)   (Schools/Carnivals)
Gwen Wood(née Downer)   (New Inn/Numerous others)

Although others may appear for which no direct acknowledgment is made, I trust the donors will accept my grateful thanks. There are bound to be disappointments through material that I so eagerly sought not appearing within the book due to space limitations. However hopefully the items concerned, which will be lodged with the Swanmore Society, will not be wasted, and could well feature in future exhibitions of village life in the twentieth century.

The help of Doug Braund on the computerisation front and Gloria Atkinson-Carter with her administrative expertise have been invaluable in bringing the project to fruition.

Finally, and most importantly, I must thank my wife Joan for her immense patience over the last six years while I have assembled the material both for this book and the Swanmore Roll of Honour.

Keith Harrington

Introduction
by Pam Evans and Keith Harrington

After the declaration of war on September the 3rd 1939, King George VI said "There may be dark days ahead and war can no longer be confined to the battlefield....". The effects of the war proved to be sweeping, impacting on the economy, health, education, housing, employment, and family life. The emotional and psychological well-being of individuals and communities was placed under enormous strain.

In 1939, Swanmore was a parish of approximately 1220 people, and covered about 2357 acres, mostly used to grow wheat, barley, oats and roots. The village had a Church and Methodist Chapel, a Parish Reading and Recreation Room, a British Legion Hall, four public houses, several small shops, including a cycle dealer and boot repairers, and a post office. *(Kelly's Directory, 1939)*. There was a small-scale family-run brick and tile makers employing a few people, but most of the population were employed in agriculture or on the surrounding estates.

Swanmore is situated about 13 miles to the NW of Portsmouth and to the NE of Southampton, both of which cities played a large role in the war. Swanmore is only about five miles from Southwick, the strategic headquarters from which D-Day was planned, and very close to Droxford station where Churchill had his famous meeting on the platform with other Heads of State in June 1944. It is therefore in the middle of an area that saw much wartime activity, some of which had a knock-on effect in Swanmore.

However, there was much less impact on Swanmore's residents from the effects of war than on town and city dwellers. There were no major air raids on Swanmore itself and only a few bombs fell locally, including some on the nearby Meon Valley railway which was used for troop and ammunition movements *(Stone, 1996, p.69)*. There was none of the devastation to landscape with loss of lives, homes and utilities that was suffered by those who endured the blitz *(Calder, 1969)*. The people of Swanmore had to conform to various regulations such as the blackout; the Church bells were silenced; gas masks were issued; road signs and finger posts were removed *(Calder, 1969, p.121)* and acres of parkland were ploughed and planted with crops.

Night after night, when the air raids were at their height and it was the turn of Southampton or Portsmouth to be blitzed, the red glow of the cities burning could be seen from Swanmore, with explosions as bombs fell. Southampton's city centre was almost obliterated as it was a strategic target for German bombers with all its docks, troop movements and factories on vital war work, including the one manufacturing Spitfires *(Calder, 1969, pp.160-1, 206-18)*. Portsmouth was also a prime target, mainly as the home of the Royal Navy with the Naval Dockyard, ammunition stores, shipbuilding and repair facilities, etc. *(Calder, 1969, pp.206, 209-10, 218-9)*.

At the beginning of the war some children and mothers with babies had been evacuated from Portsmouth and Southampton and billeted in various local villages, including Swanmore *(Calder on South coast evacuation, p.128)*. With the advent of the blitz, there was a mass exodus from these and other cities in a phenomenon known as "trekking" *(Calder, 1969,*

3

p.217-20). Families left Southampton and Portsmouth before dark and trekked with a few possessions to surrounding safer areas. Many of those with family connections in Swanmore came to this area. A few families rented empty houses, e.g., in the neighbouring parish of Shedfield, and friends and relatives would come out from the cities each night and bed down on spare floor space before returning to work in the city at daybreak *(Emery, 1991, pp.69, 70).* "My husband was stationed in Portsmouth and he found me a place in a little village outside the town" *(quoted in Harrison, 1976, p.151).*

The number of evacuees in Swanmore was never enough to overwhelm local resources and there was little disruption to the normal working of the village school. During part of the war, some local schools shared their premises with bombed-out schools from towns, and usually each school had either the mornings or the afternoons. Educational standards inevitably fell *(Emery, 1991, p.41).*
Here, as elsewhere in rural Hampshire, there were some Land Army girls who took over the agricultural duties of men who were away fighting and to boost production of food crops and livestock. There were changes to what was grown locally, with many more vegetables grown for home consumption and for troops. Two enigmatic crops were harvested for use in munitions: cucumbers and horse chestnuts, although it is not clear in what manner they were utilised *(Emery, 1991, p.70).*

Rationing was probably less of a problem in rural areas such as Swanmore. Gardens were larger and there was an existing ethos of families growing their own fruit and vegetables. Many people kept a pig and a few chickens, and there was much exchange and barter of food commodities, not available to the average city dweller. Many people had a well for drinking water, and Swanmore did not have mains drainage and a limited gas supply. There was therefore less reliance on public utilities than in urban areas, and non-existent supplies could not be disrupted. Also, the rural population relied less heavily on public transport and on amenities such as theatres and cinemas for entertainment.

On the home front, the Civil Defence force, Auxiliary Firefighters, the Home Guard and the Women's Voluntary Service were drawn from all strata of society, although in reality few people from the working classes achieved positions of rank in any of these bodies.

Thus, from a personal viewpoint, it could be argued that the lives of Swanmore's inhabitants were altered far less and in different ways from those of British people in the cities closely affected by the war and especially the blitz.

Surviving records of organised bodies within the village reinforce this viewpoint and although the School, Scout and Women's Institute log books do have various references to the hostilities, the Parish Council and the Parochial Church Council make hardly any mention of the war. The two last named bodies, the most important administrative organisations within Swanmore, devote their time to entirely internal matters such as the upkeep of footpaths, unblocking of drainage systems, hedge-cutting, and harvest thanksgiving services. The Chairman of the Parish Council at the outbreak of war Major Harold Inglis of Hill Place resigned in 1941 to rejoin the army having already been awarded the DSO and MC in what was then referred to as The Great War (1914 - 1918).

Major Maurice Raymond Portal.

It is conceivable that the formation of the separate Invasion Committee under the chairmanship of Mrs Ethel Portal of Holywell House, wife of Major Maurice Portal, DSO, perhaps enabled other organisations to function almost normally. The Invasion Committee War Book, which is reproduced within this volume, details the extensive planning undertaken by the Committee.

Following the breaking up of the Hill Place and Swanmore Park estates in 1916 and 1935 respectively, the balance of power in the local squirearchy could arguably have been seen as shifting to Holywell where the Portals had resided since 1917. During the crucial World War II period, while Swanmore Park housed Timothy Whites' southern packaging operation, Holywell continued to function as a country estate.

The events and social changes that occurred in the aftermath of the war probably also had less impact on Swanmore than elsewhere. There was no significant unemployment or housing shortages and there were no major educational issues. There were probably similar changes in social trends such as birth, marriage and divorce rates, although these have not been ascertained.

At the end of the war, thirteen more names were added to the village war memorial and all those killed in action would have been known by and related to many families who still have roots in Swanmore today. Mrs Portal had laid the wreath on behalf of the Royal British Legion at the original dedication service in 1921 following the ending of World War I in 1918.

Not surprisingly for such a small parish, there has been little written evidence for the effects of the Second World War on the local population. However, there is a wealth of information in the memories of many of the inhabitants, and hopefully this book will bring these alive for present and future generations.

Major Portal and Countess Howe
at Idsworth Park Dog Trials, November 1936.

5

Holywell House, the home of Major and Mrs Maurice Portal. - photograph from Country Life, 18th February 1999

Hill Place (from the estate sale brochure in 1916).
At the outbreak of the war Hill Place was the residence of Major Harold Inglis DSO, MC, JP.

*Holywell House, the home of Major and Mrs Maurice Portal, from circa 1920 - 1960
An article in the Hampshire Telegraph, 20th May 1971.*

7

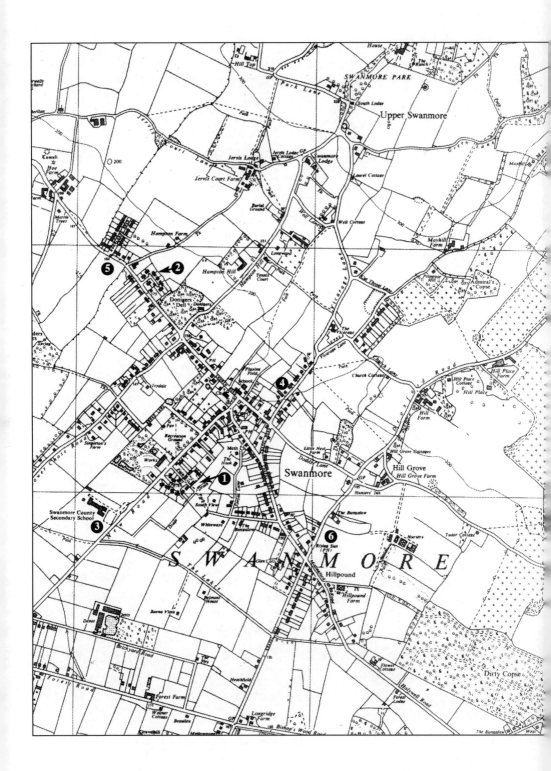

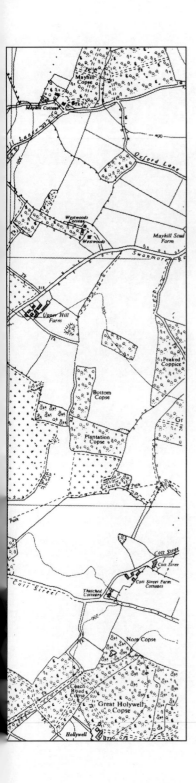

Editors Note

Section 1 on the left, Page 8 includes the more populated areas of the village whilst section 2 on this page details the more rural easterly parts of the parish.

Post war changes are noted as follows
1. Spring Vale, development commenced 1952
2. Donigers Close, development commenced 1955
3. Swamore Secondary School opened 1961

Second World War Bomb sites are marked at
4. Bucketts Farm in Vicarage Lane.
5. Swanmore Road (opposite Morelands Rd)
6. Hill Pound near to the Bungalow

Census figures for the village show a population of 1218 in 1931 which had risen to 1429 by 1951. There was no census in 1941, but see page 131.

This document is included as it shows current road names and should help those readers from outside the village to identify places mentioned.

R. Harvey (Hon.-Sec.)   C. White.   E. Allen.   G. Joyce.   H. Martin. (Hon.-Treas.)   F. Clark. (Committee)

A. Gibson. (Committee)   R. Allen.   W. Emery.   L. Joyce.   W. Harris.   W. Watson (Capt.)   R. Barnes.

E. Emery.   J. Hack.

SWANMORE F.C. WINNERS PINK CUP 1930.

Swanmore Methodist Church Sunday School outing c.1932.
Back: Iris Willoughby, Joyce Edney, Mr Edney, Mrs Clem Butcher, Mrs Peachey
Middle: Marjorie Butcher, Doris Willoughby (later Fittall), Alma Edney (later Parsons)
Front: Jeff Butcher

Brownies at the Vicarage. Circa 1935
Back: Evelyn McNally, Phyllis West, Mary Smith, Gwen Downer, Mary Hughes
Front: Elsie George, Gladys Kirby, Audrey Dewey, Joan West

11

Swimmers at a Guide camp circa 1935

Back L-R Standing: Marjorie Hack (Durley), third from right Phyllis Hall (Swanmore), extreme right: Annie Downer (Swanmore)
Front L-R Sitting: Elsie Hutching (Durley), Jean Houghton (Durley) now Jean Terry of Swanmore Rd), Daphne Clark (Bishops Waltham),
Trixie Strick (Swanmore), Jean Edney (Swanmore), Phyllis Strick (Swanmore)

Swanmore Scouts in 1938 after an informal football match.
Back: R Tudgey, Peter Rowsell and Harry Grace (visitors), R Fry
Middle: F Terry, P Carpenter, J H Clutterbuck, R Mockler, R Gibson
Front: H Burford, J Wellstead, J Clarke, A Houghton

Swanmore Cubs camp, 1939.
Back: R Snook, C Parsons, P Kemp, J Jacobs, R Crouch
Middle: C George, Mr Newman, Skipper (J.H. Clutterbuck), E Titheridge, P Carpenter
Front: G Curley, Ron Gibson, L Joyce, G Crouch, P Parsons

Silver Jubilee of George V, 6th May 1935
Left to right: Kathleen Watson (Ireland), Mary Whitaker (Boudicea),Molly Watson (Wales)
and John Watson (Scotland).

Silver Jubilee of George V, 6th May 1935 - probably Peter Parsons on the horse.

Mid 1930's Carnival - William "Bluebell" Adams and Cyril White.

Silver Jubilee of George V, 6th May 1935 - Jim Parsons on a tractor.

Swanmore Primary School - circa 1935

Back: Peter Carpenter, Keith Kerton, Ray Sylvester, Don Watson, Sue Goater, Phyllis Coleman, Eileen Gibson, Gwen Downer, Joan Sales, Aileen Dewey, Alma Springall, Audrey Dewey. 2nd from back: Ron Vincent, Percy Cole, George Goater, Les Wooldridge, Ron Crook, Winnie Purdue, Linda Reed, Dorothy Mouland, Mildred Didymus, Alma Edney, Jean Edney, Lily Kirby, Mrs Whitaker. 3rd row: Frank Terry, Victor Pane, Monty Hibbard, George Adams, Harry Merrit, Hilda Gamblin, Muriel Smith, Dora Newland, Doris Willoughby, Emily Wearn, Marjorie Butcher, Florrie Springle, Jim Bound 4th from back: Fred Terry, Walter McNally, Ron Moore, Harold Burford, Trevor Newland, Roland Jeffery, Eileen Gibson, Pansy Richardson, Phyllis West, Barbara McNally, Rita Reed, Elsie George, Jean Kerton Front: Ray Saunders, Donald Hibbard, Ted Smith, Ray Mockler, Alfred Day, ? Wooldridge, Tom Tier, Gladys Tier, Pat Springle, Kath Bound, Alice Pink

Swanmore Primary School, 1937.

Back: Jo Chapman, Margaret Marsh, Georgia Locke, Cecilia Featherstone, Betty Parsons, Barbara Burford, Barbara Kemp, Vera Tribbeck, Grace Joyce, Evelyn Messam. Next: Stanley Hibberd, Michael Moore, Maurice Johnson, Alan Horner, Arthur Tier, David Messam, Phil Gomer, Walter Trivett, Eric Bound, Philip Cole, Nelson Upfield. Sitting: Alan Fry, Ray Gibson, John Elliot, Maureen Newton, Margaret Emery, Peggy Watson, ?, ?, ? Front: Eric Pothecary, Fred Clarke, Tony Crouch, Arthur Emery.

St Barnabas and the Methodist Church
by Peter R Watkins

When war began, church life was at a low ebb, something of which the Vicar [the Revd Alan Brown] seemed to be aware. His monthly letters in the Parish Magazine bemoan the decline of Christian civilisation and suggest that Swanmore's contribution to remedying this situation would be to attend church in greater numbers and more often, though he can have had little hope that either would happen. Attendance of only 83 at Easter communion services in 1942 was lower than in any year since records began in 1897.

Apart from Sunday and weekday services, the only regular church activity was the Mothers' Union. Helen Brown, the Vicar's wife, was its president and felt a pastoral responsibility for its members. In the autumn of 1939 she hoped 'to meet all MU members in their homes in the next three months'.

Church officials—wardens, sidesmen, sexton and verger—were predominantly male, though from 1940-42 St Barnabas' had, in Mrs Beckett, its first woman churchwarden, who sadly died in office. The church was no longer, as it had been during the First World War, the focus of village life. No lists of those serving in the forces or of casualties appear in the parish magazine. When the Vicar appealed for the names of those serving, so that he could add their names to the prayer list, he received one. "Is it shyness?", he wrote, "Is it disbelief in the power of prayer? Is it carelessness? Whatever it is, it is not a healthy sign".

The Vicar did not enjoy good health, and this, combined with continuing dissatisfaction with the Vicarage, led to his resignation in September 1942 to become Vicar of Ampfield. The PCC had views about the new Vicar: he should be 'a moderate churchman and not advanced in years'. Mr Brown was presented with 'a bundle of notes, about £40, that had been collected in the parish'.

The new Vicar met the parish's specifications. Edward Stephen Wakefield was educated at the London College of Divinity and ordained priest in 1939. He served curacies at St. Luke's, Wimbledon and Christ Church, Croydon before coming to Swanmore, still scarcely 30, with a wife and daughter, Rosemary. Their son, Christopher, was born in April 1944. Edward Wakefield's brief incumbency of three and a half years saw the beginning of a renewal of confidence.

Revd Edward Stephen Wakefield, Vicar of Swanmore 1943-6.

The new format of the parish magazine symbolised a more contemporary approach, with the fresh air let in to what had become a rather old-fashioned publication. The cover of the old magazine, adopted in 1904, was filled with fussy gothic detail. The new magazine was note-book size, the cover design simpler and the type face contemporary. Inside, the tone was less pessimistic, more outward looking and down-to-earth. Room was made for parish news, though it was still a church magazine with a relatively small circulation.

St Barnabas Church interior in the1920s.

As a young man, the new Vicar was keenly aware of the needs of children and young people, and held a diocesan responsibility for advising the Bishop on youth work. A Youth Club for those over 14 was started in 1943 and soon had a membership of over 30. There were also girls' and boys' clubs, with a variety of activities, all using the Parish Room on different nights. The Sunday School was renamed Children's (later Young People's) Church, and elected its own churchwardens, sidesmen and council.

Edward Wakefield's ministry also saw a growth of cooperation between the parish church and the Methodist chapel, assisted no doubt by the personal rapport between the Vicar and the Revd James Lindsay, minister of the Droxford Methodist circuit from 1939 to 1945. In March 1943, the two clergy called a meeting to discuss the religious education of young people, at which Mr Lindsay took the chair and the Vicar spoke. Later in the year, a joint Harvest Festival service was planned. Enquiries were made as to whether the Bishop would allow a nonconformist to preach at St Barnabas. He would, if the PCC did not object. The PCC 'enthusiastically agreed', and James Lindsay became the first free churchman to preach in St Barnabas. His ministry was 'much appreciated' and it was agreed that a joint service should be an annual event.

Swanmore Methodist Church interior - a wartime Harvest Festival.

In September 1944, the Methodists were represented when the new burial ground was consecrated by the Bishop. Joint services marked the closing stages of the war and the peace celebrations. In June 1944, a

Revd and Mrs Lindsay.
The Revd James Lindsay was minister of the Methodist Church 1939-45.

service was held after the D Day landings, with soldiers awaiting embarkation present in church, which was so full that extra chairs were needed. Joint services were also held in May 1945 to mark the end of the war in Europe and on 9th June 1946, when thanksgiving services for victory were held in connection with official celebrations countrywide. Meanwhile the church bells, silent since 1939, their use reserved to warn of impending invasion, were rung again in June 1943 when the threat had passed.

A History of St Barnabas Church, Swanmore, 1845-1995 by *Peter R Watkins*

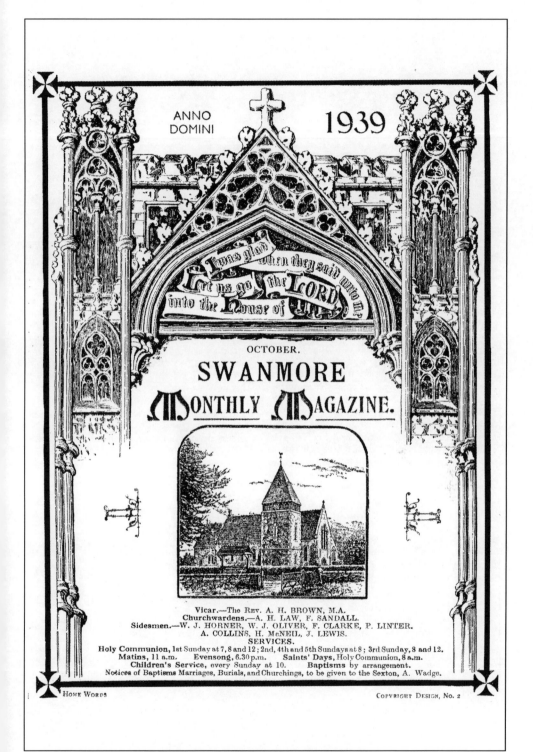

ANNO DOMINI

1939

I was glad when they said unto me,
Let us go into the House of the LORD.

OCTOBER.

SWANMORE MONTHLY MAGAZINE.

Vicar.—The Rev. A. H. BROWN, M.A.
Churchwardens.—A. H. LAW, F. SANDALL.
Sidesmen.—W. J. HORNER, W. J. OLIVER, F. CLARKE, P. LINTER.
A. COLLINS, H. McNEIL, J. LEWIS.
SERVICES.
Holy Communion, 1st Sunday at 7, 8 and 12 ; 2nd, 4th and 5th Sundays at 8 ; 3rd Sunday, 8 and 12.
Matins, 11 a.m.   Evensong, 6.30 p.m.   Saints' Days, Holy Communion, 8 a.m.
Children's Service, every Sunday at 10.   Baptisms by arrangement.
Notices of Baptisms Marriages, Burials, and Churchings, to be given to the Sexton, A. Wadge.

HOME WORDS   COPYRIGHT DESIGN, No. 2

Swanmore Parish Magazine cover, October 1939.

21

My dear People,—

I wish I were writing to you in happier circumstances, but we are in the war and it seems quite clear that we have got to carry it through. But there is a moral which I want to draw. The fate of Poland has horrified the world. It was begun by Germany and is being finished by Russia. Official Germany has long since abandoned any profession of practical Christianity, and Russia denies that there is a God at all. And it is perfectly clear that all those facts are bound together. There cannot be justice or freedom or any of the virtues which make human life possible unless they spring from faith in God and obedience to God. Christian civilization, imperfect though it is, is a real thing, and as its name implies it springs from Christ and has been won for us by generations of Christian warriors. If it is to continue and if our nation is to fulfil its high calling, God still needs his servants. This means that he needs you. You must pray : you must worship in His house where He promises to meet you and where He speaks to His family : and in your daily life you must try as never before to let Him control your every thought and action. This is the real war and this is the means of victory. Be definite about it.

Your sincere Friend,
A. H. BROWN.

We should like, in Church, a list of the names of all those serving in the Forces, so that they may be prayed for. Will you help to compile it either by giving the names to me or by writing them on the paper to be found in the Church Porch.

The Carnival Committee has made the following grants from its surplus :—Nursing Association, £2 ; Parish Room, £2 ; Boys' Club, £3 ; Girl Guides, £4 ; Boy Scouts, £4. All will doubtless be extremely grateful.

MOTHERS' UNION.

Our first meeting of the M.U. year will be held on Tuesday, October 3, at 3 o'clock. We will first of all have a short service in Church, with an address from the Vicar, and we will then go to the Parish Room for our usual yearly business meeting. The new committee will be elected, and finance for the year reviewed.

The M.U. Sale of work on September 21 was disappointing so far as attendance and takings were concerned. There was only a mere handful of members there, and they nobly shared out the work of selling, tea, etc., between them. But very few mothers came to buy. On the other hand one cannot praise too highly the beautiful work which members had done, and much of it should have found ready purchasers very easily. We hope to have a stall on October 3, when you will all have an opportunity to see all that has been made.

Our first meeting will be held in the new atmosphere created by war, and we must, through constant prayer and God's guidance, find out how we M.U. members can best adapt ourselves to the new conditions so that we and our Society may be a source of strength and comfort to others.

HELEN BROWN.

BAPTISM.

Sept. 10. David, son of Alfred and Maimie Wadge.

WEDDINGS.

July 9. Frederick George Weavil and Verona Lottie Pink.
Sept. 16. Cyril Edward Perks and Gwendoline Mollie May Carter.

BURIALS.

June 22. Willie Didymus, aged 70.
,, 27. Stephen Kill, aged 75.
July 21. Noah Charles Ralph, aged 47.
,, 26. Charles Hibdige, aged 49.
Sept. 21. Annie Wright Brixey, aged 90.

Swanmore Parish Magazine - Oct 1939.

This year there will be no official observance of the Two Minutes' Silence on Armistice Day. I have consulted with the British Legion and others and we shall not have a service at the Memorial on the day itself. But the Legion will parade on Sunday, November 12, and we shall have a silence in Church then. The Legion will place its wreath on the Memorial on the way to Church.

This arrangement in no way means that the Fallen of 1914–1918 are forgotten. But the circumstances of this year demand a change, and for some years past Armistice Day has meant a looking forward as well as backward. The need could not be too strongly put for a full Church on this day as an act both of remembrance and dedication. And if there is no official Silence on November 11, let us, as far as we may, keep it privately.

The war goes on and no one knows for how long. As I write there is great activity in Germany, which may result either in a new " Peace Move " or a military offensive. Hitler's pilgrimage to Moscow was a fatal step for him, and men are rightly already beginning to wonder how Europe can be settled after the war is over. The spiritual battle will be even more fraught with vital consequences than the military one. And if you call yourself a Christian you are playing into the hands of paganism and tyranny if you do not now swell the forces of God by open and eager allegiance to the faith you profess. We are optimistic about the military war. There is less immediate ground for optimism as to the spiritual warfare. Yet it is on this that our destinies hang.

I want to add a personal note. Through the Church Council and with the help of others outside it several internal improvements to the Vicarage have just been completed. Many of you deplore the Vicarage's size, but the things that have been done make a very great difference to its manageability, and my wife and I want most sincerely to thank the Council and all others who have helped towards it.

The Parish Room Jumble Sale will be on Friday, November 17, at 6 p.m. Will those who have articles to give—and we are in greater need this year—let me know of it, and if possible the things are needed at the Parish Room the day before. We hope to improve matters this year by having some competitions and side-shows.

MOTHERS' UNION.

Owing to restrictions necessary when we are at war we cannot hope to keep to our M.U. year as planned. Rationing, light, and petrol restrictions make it impossible to give our usual Old Folks' Tea to Droxford Institution, and we shall have to devise something in its place so that the old people will not be completely deprived of their annual festivity. The same applies to our own M.U. Christmas Tea. Then, too, speakers had been arranged up to next June, but most of them are too far away to come under the new conditions. We are fortunate in being near enough to have Mrs. Martin, of Sledfield, to speak to us at the November meeting, and in December we shall have the great pleasure of welcoming our Diocesan President, Mrs. Carpenter-Garnier, who will give us an address and lead us in Intercessions.

At our yearly meeting in October the three vacancies on the M.U. Committee (which has another year to run before re-election) were filled, by vote, by Mrs. French, Mrs. Wainwright and Mrs. Whitborne. The other four members are Mrs. Law (Secretary), Mrs. Stubbington, Mrs. Vincent and myself, *ex officio*. Mrs. Wainwright has kindly consented to act as Treasurer. We welcome the new members warmly.

The Swanmore Mothers' Union has suffered a great loss in the resignation of Mrs. Collins from the committee. We can never be grateful enough for the ungrudging, tireless way in which she has worked for the M.U.—never sparing herself, keeping our finances together, and setting an example to us all of unselfish service to a worthy cause. She has always been of the greatest help to me, personally, since I came to the parish, and I miss her presence at our meetings more than I can say. Only ill-health has made her lay down her work, and I hope that it will not be long before she is at least strong enough to resume her attendance at the meetings. We shall all be glad to have her among us again.

Important.—Beginning in November our M.U. meetings will start at **2.30** instead of 3 (for the winter months), and the first quarter of an hour of each meeting will be devoted to Intercession.

HELEN BROWN.

BAPTISM.
Oct. 15. Janice Mary, daughter of Richard and Ethel Roberts.

BURIALS.
Sept. 27. Isabella Reeves, aged 28.
Oct. 24. Lottie Lillywhite, aged 57.

COLLECTION.	£	s.	d.
Oct. 8. Winchester Hospital	5	6	7

Swanmore Parish Magazine - Nov 1939.

We have just suffered the first casualties of the war and we give our sympathy to Mrs. Bath and Mr. and Mrs. Willing. We do not forget either those who anxiously wait for news of the missing, and who are meeting anxiety with such courage. We sympathize too with those who have been turned out of their homes in Vicarage Lane, though we are supremely thankful that the bomb did not explode as it fell. In fact, though there have been disasters, yet in comparison with many other places we have every cause for gratitude. Our duty is plainly to carry on as normally as we can. Ordinary friendships, ordinary worship, these are the things that give strength and meaning to life, and by taking our part in them we both give and receive strength.

You will see that new work is being done at the School to give protection from blast and splinters. This, with the work already done in the lobbies, should give every reasonable safety. Parents are consequently urged to see that their children attend School as they always have done. Nothing is better for their nerves than to live a normal, orderly life, and if they sometimes miss their sleep the discipline of School should have a quietening effect. At the same time have a thought for the teachers. If the children are not up to the mark it makes the teacher's work very much harder, and they have a great responsibility.

I think there are probably some who have run out of Duplex Envelopes and have not asked for more. Please remember that the Duplex Scheme is the foundation of our financial building, based as it is on the principle that we give what we owe, and even if your contribution is only a small one its place is an essential one. I have a plentiful supply of envelopes and I want you to ask for some.

BAPTISMS.

Sept. 1. Anthony Colin, son of Frank and Edith Gibson.

,, 22. Alfred Frank, son of Frederick and Verona Weavil.

,, ,, Robert, son of Edward and Ethel Lane.

COLLECTION.

Sept. 22. Winchester Hospital £4 19 5

Swanmore Parish Magazine - Oct 1940.

Editor's Note

Before the end of 1946, both ministers had left the village to take up other posts. In the case of the Revd Edward Wakefield, who was Swanmore's youngest vicar of the 20th century, undoubtedly a major reason for his leaving would have been the dilapidated state of the Victorian Vicarage, which had also led to the early departure of several of his predecessors. He went on to become the Rector of Pewsey and a Canon of Salisbury Cathedral.

SWANMORE PARISH CHURCH.

❖■❖❖■❖❖

VICAR.

THE REV. E. S. WAKEFIELD, B.Sc.

CHURCHWARDENS.

H. C. WAINWRIGHT.   Major H. J. INGLIS.

SIDESMEN.

H. AINSLEY, F. CLARKE, A. COLLINS, A. H. LAW,
H. MARTIN, A. TILBURY, A. VINCENT.

ORGANIST.

C. H. RENYARD.

Notices of Baptisms, Weddings, Burials and Churchings, to be given
to the Sexton, A. J. Vincent.

CALENDAR.

Sunday, Holy Communion at 8.0 a.m.
Mattins at 11.0 a.m.
Evensong at 6.30 p.m.
Children's Church at 10.0 a.m.
1st and 3rd Sundays, Holy Communion at 12.
2nd Sunday, Baptisms at 2.30 p.m.

BAPTISM.

May 13. Julia Eileen Oliver.

WEDDING.

May 15. Peter Bernall Williams to Phyllis Esther Strick.

BURIAL.

April 27. Ellen Lawrence, aged 88 years.

THE VICARAGE, SWANMORE,
May, 1945.

MY DEAR FRIENDS,—

Great things have happened since last I wrote to you. We rejoice in the triumph of our Forces over those of the enemy. Yet, as we have reminded ourselves so often before the great event took place, we face an even bigger problem, that of winning the peace. We lost it last time, and it is not an easy task that is now before us. We've got to face up to the conditions we've found in Europe, and we must remember that both there, and at home, only the Christian way of life will really solve the problems. As far as you and I are concerned, this means that we must see to it that our own lives are Christian, and that Christian standards pervade our homes, our village and our nation. We shall throw away the victory that has been won at such tremendous cost, if we leave God out of account, and thus we shall become literally godless.

One big event in our village serves to put the other side of the picture to us. A hundred years ago there were people living where we live in this village who gave money to build our Church. They wanted to make it more possible to worship, for a journey to Droxford was no easier then than it is now. They found the money and built the Church. It is our inheritance. This month we are celebrating its Centenary. Let us use the special Services as a time to re-dedicate ourselves to God for the great tasks ahead. Let us leave a worthy memorial of our day and generation—not this time in a building of stone, but in a building of Christian character and tradition. Let us mark this year by seeing to it that with God's help we will lay the foundations of a Christian way of life in our village. In simple terms, this means that each one of us will see to it that we give to God first place in our lives —that every activity of our life is centred upon Him.

As an outward expression of this, I am suggesting that we devote part of our Centenary Fund towards a Children's Corner, a place in our Church where there will be children's books and pictures, a corner of the Church which the children will feel and know is specially their own.

Let us all use the opportunities that this month offers to demonstrate our gratitude to God for 100 years of Christian witness in our village.

Yours very sincerely,
E. S. WAKEFIELD.

PARISH NOTES AND NEWS.

Another Full Church.—One of the biggest congregations over seen in our Church marked the Day of Thanksgiving and Re-dedication to God on the Victory in Europe, Sunday, May 13. A parade, led by the men and women of the village on leave from the Services, and including every organisation in the village, assembled and marched to Church. Even the Church porch had people in it!

It is fitting to recall that the previous occasion on which the Church was full to overflowing was when the men of the Services themselves came on that memorable June morning immediately after D Day. Our service on May 13 was the sequel.

Lenten Boxes.—A total of £3 1s. 9d. was received from seventeen boxes, and this amount goes to the Church Missionary Society.

Confirmation.—At the Church of SS. Peter and Paul, Fareham, on May 16, the following candidates were confirmed by Bishop Kitching,

Swanmore School

Ernest Frank Whitaker, head-master of Swanmore Church of England School from 1913 to 1942.

The Headmaster, Ernest Whitaker, who had been appointed at the start of the First World War, retired on the 31st January 1942. His successor was Margaret Belbin, the last Head and only woman to hold that post at the all-age school. Miss Belbin, who was in her 20s when appointed, was to remain in the position for over 20 years.

Considerable disruption of pupils' studies occurred, particularly during the early war years, and many attendance hours were lost with pupils helping with the war effort through harvesting, fruit picking, etc.

However, as Miss Belbin's headship developed, the horizons of pupils were gradually widened, and pupils such as Vera Tribbeck and June Clarkson were among those who gained admission to Winchester High School for Girls.

The old Infant School.

War-Time School Days
by Vera Tribbeck and Mary Burgess (née Tribbeck)

I was six years old and attending Swanmore Infants School when war broke out in 1939, and my sister Mary was almost eight and by now at the main primary school. Memories are now sketchy from those days but a few things stand out. Some evacuees arrived and I just remember two girls and a boy being billeted with Mrs Robinson at Winsford Cottage, the house next door. Also some teachers from Gosport lived at what is now Greenfields Lodge, next to the school.

26

Swanmore Primary School painting, 7th June 1963 by Sydney Maiden. Although painted some time after the war, the building looked much like this during the war (except for the tree, which should be further to the right).

For a time we used the school in the mornings only and the evacuees used it in the afternoon. Later we had classes in the British Legion Hall and the Methodist Church school room. School was disrupted at times because of air raids, and we sometimes went in later or were sent home. Nature walks to Upper Swanmore were organised by a teacher, Miss Blunden, in order to take the children away from the school and the centre of the village, for safety! The sounds of the war are still vivid – the warning siren coming from Bishops Waltham – the drone of aircraft overhead – "Are they enemy planes?" – gun fire, dog-fights, then the relief of the all-clear signal. Later on, the frightening, monotonous drone of doodle-bugs, still buzzing in your head long after they had gone.

I can remember the day Mum had to take us to the Parish Room to collect these peculiar gas masks that were in cardboard boxes with a string attached. She made us nice shoulder bags out of grey flannel and we had to take them with us at all times. Gas-mask drill was carried out regularly by the class teacher and woe betide anyone who blew raspberries (very tempting). When my class was at one end of the British Legion Hall and the top class the other end, the big boys were caned for producing these noises, by the headmaster Mr Whitaker, who was in a bit of a rage. Ink wells sat on the top of tables, as there were no desks, and these were knocked over – what a mess – we younger children thought it was hilarious and a great diversion.

School milk was introduced during the war and our mothers were asked to provide us with a mug that would hold one-third of a pint. Mr Frederick Marsh wheeled his churn up Swanmore Hill and ladled out the appropriate measurement. Sometimes the milk was quite warm as it came "straight from the cows"! Also the odd cow's hair would stray into a mug! This happened to me on one occasion but I forgave Mr Marsh, as I loved his delicious creamy milk. School dinners arrived in metal containers from Portchester in 1944. We paraded,

27

crocodile fashion, down New Road to the British Legion Hall where the meals were served by some of my friends' mothers; I can recall Mrs Newton and Mrs Emery. There were others I am sure. Being a fussy child, I wasn't keen on the gristly meat and powdery custard, as I saw it, but no doubt the best that could be provided and probably quite nutritious for some children who had poor diets due to rationing and lack of money. I remember many children who seemed very poor and had few clothes to wear.

Paper was very short. I was fond of drawing but there was no sign of any proper drawing paper. I cut the end papers from my reading books or painted on the plain side of cereal packets. At school we did have exercise books issued by the Southampton Education Committee, bearing safety regulations printed on the back cover. I still possess a few of mine, kept by my mother, covering the period 1939 to 1941. The only mention of the war is in a 1941 book when I was eight years old. In a letter-writing exercise, I was writing an imaginary letter to an uncle in Canada and said, "Now the war is on I cannot come and see you. I hope the war will be over by next year. It is so hateful." I seem to remember squared paper for doing sums. Dark grey paper was used for drawing with poor pastels or wax

crayons. Art education was practically NIL anyway – we just occasionally drew daffodils and primroses. No craftwork was done; although there was grubby plasticine in the infants' school, I don't remember what we did with it! However, we had good grounding in the 3 Rs and read a few classics with Mrs Whitaker.

Life outside school was mainly spent playing with friends on Saturdays and holiday times. Sunday was always a family day. Sunday School or church with mother, table games in the afternoons, evening walks with

Edith Willing (of the Rising Sun) made this cake for children of the village in the war.

both parents in the summer. Outings were very restricted; the beaches were wired up for a lot of the war time. We played in the fields and in our gardens and learned to do "dog paddle" and catch minnows in the river at Mislingford. It was difficult to cater for children's parties but our mothers were very skilled at making delicious cakes from next to nothing. Mum's chocolate cakes were very popular and who will forget Mrs Watson's coffee kisses! The British Legion and other village people organised an annual party for all the village children. We had a tea, a gift and an entertainment in the hall. Very exciting. Mr & Mrs Willing, from the Rising Sun, were very good at parties and hilarious shows. Pop Willing, as he was called, once performed a "Chamber Concert": rows of metal chamber pots strung across the stage, which he tickled with a drum-stick and a brush (I think!). I can say that neither my sister nor I felt any great fear because our parents and aunties showed none and just carried on with their work as usual.

Cecil ('Pop') Willing of the Rising Sun.

J & M Tribbeck's Bakery and Store
by Vera Tribbeck and Mary Burgess (née Tribbeck)

James Tribbeck was featured in the Invasion Committee War Book as emergency baker and committee member. His bakery and grocery store was at Hill Pound Crossroads.

It was extremely difficult running a small village business during the war because of many shortages and regulations. It was probably assumed that, if you had a food busi-

Mary, James and Edith Tribbeck outside their house in the 1920s.

ness, you were personally able to have all that you needed. Nothing was further from the truth – my dad and his three sisters, who ran the business, would move heaven and earth to supply their customers, often depriving themselves. When the suppliers, Page & Sons of Southampton, were bombed and put out of action for a while, there was very little to sell or provide customers with their correct rations. This problem and the financial worries affected the health of the eldest family members, Aunt Mary Tribbeck (known as Polly) suffering permanent loss of memory.

The bread production was the most successful, flour coming from Botley Mills without any problems. However there was a time when no sugar was available and Dad's popular lard

James Tribbeck delivering bread.

cakes (not called 'lardy' then!) had to be made with black treacle. Delicious actually! I would dare to say that locally-made bread and home-grown vegetables were the staple diet of the people in Swanmore.

Deliveries of bread and groceries were made to all parts of the village and, being single-handed, Dad had to bake the bread in the mornings and deliver in the afternoons and evenings. During winter evenings, when lights were required on the van, the blackout regulations were such that metal slatted covers had to be fixed over the headlamps. Imagine how difficult it became to negotiate the narrow lanes of Upper Swanmore, including the icy and treacherous Damson Hill, with such dim lighting.

People like my father were home-front heroes, in my eyes.

Every minute of the day was occupied. On his one afternoon off, Wednesdays, he spent all the time in the gardens, growing potatoes and other veg. – in our garden and that of my elderly aunt and cousin, Fanny and Dorothy Newnham, who lived on the other side of the road: nine family members in all. At night he was frequently on fire-watching duties as the leading Fire Watch Officer for Hill Pound. In his team were:

Mrs Robinson – later a Red Cross worker in France
Mr Bert Underwood
Mr Willing of The Rising Sun
Mr Edgar Watson
Mr Gordy Sylvester
Mr Arch Pink

*Bert and Mabel Underwood
and their niece at their house,
Glen Cottage, in the 1950s.*

Our bungalow (Kasvin) was the depot for certain items such as cream for burns, gas masks and a stirrup pump; a white card with red wording was permanently displayed in the sitting room window that faced the road to indicate the items that could be obtained. The stirrup pumps were tested in the grounds of The Rising Sun on Sundays.

On Sunday evenings the family would sit together cutting coupons from ration books and getting them ready for Dad to take to the Food Office at Bishops Waltham Institute on Monday mornings. Another task!

The last straw was the introduction of bread rationing, which only lasted for a short time. I remember my mother had to go on the round to help Dad with collecting the coupons. I don't believe it proved to be practicable – too much of a burden to administer.

*Glen Cottage, the home of Bert and Mabel Underwood,
in the 1950s. It was where Glendale now is.*

30

The Rising Sun.

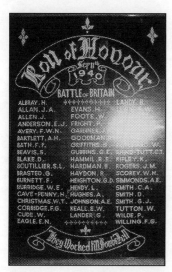

Cecil ('Pop') Willing in the Rising Sun.

Pubs

The Rising Sun

Swanmore was on the old coaching road to London, and the stable for the change of horses was historically at the Rising Sun Inn. At the outset of the war, the landlord was Alf Primmer. Since there was no electricity, a game of darts had to proceed by candlelight. Then early in 1940, the Willing family arrived, having previously run a pub in Margate but being Londoners by origin. The Willings quickly made their mark on the local scene, Cecil 'Pop' Willing becoming the cook to the Swanmore Home Guard unit and he often also provided entertainment for local children's parties. Sadly Pop and his wife, Edith, lost their only son, Frederick, very early in the war when the Cunliffe Owen factory, now Ford's, at Eastleigh was bombed. Frederick and another villager, Frederick Bath of Moorlands Road, were among the 52 who perished.

Roll of Honour at the Cunliffe Owen factory (now Ford's) at Eastleigh. The factory was bombed on 11th September 1940. Fred Grovner Willing's name is the last on the roll.

Fred Grovner Willing, 19, who was killed when the Cunliffe Owen factory was bombed on 11th September 1940.

The Bricklayers Arms.

The Bricklayers Arms - view from the garden.

The Bricklayers (now Brickmakers) Arms

The landlord of the 1930s Alfred Kirby returned to policing early in the war, and was replaced by George Pratt. John Watson of Shapeton, Hill Pound, who was then only 11, remembers that the pub was always popular with coach parties, particularly from the Naval Base at Portsmouth, who would make use of the Dance Hall at the rear of the building. Royal Navy ships' crests decorated the bar.

The Hunters Inn

The licensees were Mr and Mrs Eames. There was considerable competition between the Hunters and the Bricklayers for the incoming coach parties. John Watson recollects that live music was provided by Vic Hack and George (Dick) Silvester who both played the piano accordion; they were backed up by Charlie Hack on drums and Don Hibberd, triangle.

The Hunters Inn and bowling green.

The Hunters Inn, Cott Street.

The New Inn

The landlord was Walter Downer, father of Mrs Gwen Wood. The pub was divided into smaller bars; the Saloon was where the ladies were to be found, while the Public Bar with its sawdust floors was the domain of the regular male drinkers. There was a separate tap-room where games facilities were provided such as rings, darts and shove ha'penny. John Watson remembers in the immediate post war period local characters such as Bill Parsons and Bill

The New Inn.

Linter playing very competitive rings matches. The latter would shout "'prighter" (more upright) if his opponent lent too far forward when casting his ring.

The British Legion Hall - later it became the Village Hall. When this photo was taken, it was up for sale, because the new hall was being built further down New Road.

The British Legion Hall and the Parish Rooms

The British Legion Hall, built soon after World War I, stood on the site now occupied by Maxwell and St Aubyn's houses in New Road. It was well utilised during the Second World War with some school classes and many children's parties being held on the premises. However the main functions were the bar, snooker table and facilities for dancing.

The Parish Room had a Reading Room, now incorporated into Church House in Church Road, and behind this was a Dance Hall, now demolished. John Watson of Shapeton recalls as a lad playing billiards for fourpence and snooker for sixpence a time; games of darts were free. Monies raised from the various activities helped to offset the running expenses.

Parish Reading Room

Recollections of June Clarkson (née Gillard)

The Outbreak of War: 1939—War Clouds Break

I remember that the news broke on a Sunday morning, as we had had the traditional late Sunday cooked breakfast, and that remnants of it all were still on the table. As my father switched on the wireless, we were all told to "Hush", and we did indeed fall silent as he sat and listened with his head down. I have no memory of the words of the broadcast that morning, but watched him as he silently switched off the wireless and turned to go out of the door and along the path to the gate.

I ran after him and grabbed his hand and he held it tightly. I swung along beside him, out into the dusty gravel of Moorlands Road. Although only six years old, I knew that something was seriously wrong when I saw that the road, usually so peaceful and quiet on a Sunday morning, was full of other men, all standing around in groups, talking in subdued voices and looking at the ground. More of a surprise was the fact that my father, who normally had very little time to talk to the other men up the road—indeed, we hardly knew them—was going up the road to talk to them. It was all most strange and even rather frightening. I swung on my father's hand and scuffed the gravel but was told sharply, to stop and stand still. It was all very odd indeed. To me as a child, on a morning when the road was bathed in lovely Autumn sunshine, it felt all wrong. I wondered what it could all be about, but was not told.

My parents were, of course, only too aware that Poland had been invaded and over-run only days before the announcement, and that a similar fate could well await us.

Within a few days, it seemed, drapes of heavy dark material, dug out from a family chest, were hung over our windows as black-out blinds, and air-raid sirens began to wail over the countryside. Everyone, I remember, was given instructions to take cover when they heard the siren's terrifying wail and not to venture out until the All-Clear sounded. The sirens were very loud and were to warn of the approach of enemy aircraft. They were practice sirens only, to begin with, but within a year enemy aircraft were indeed flying over our towns and cities, dropping bombs on Portsmouth and Southampton, causing death and destruction.

The Battle of Britain—Summer/Winter 1940

By the summer of 1940, I was seven years old and knew a lot more about the War—I knew that we had an 'enemy' called Hitler and an enemy country called Germany. We also all knew that the 'enemy' could possibly come to Swanmore and capture us all!

That summer, seemingly every day, the air-raid sirens and all-clears filled the air with their terrifying wails. There were no hard-and-fast rules about where to go while these raids were going on—we had a 'dug-out' in the garden and initially sat down there at night when a raid was on, but when it became clear the village was not in real danger, most families just sat it out, indoors (or even out of doors!) watching the dog-fights from their gardens and back doors. We had a good aerial view of the bombing going on in the skies above Southampton and Portsmouth, and followed the smoke trails of the falling planes and barrage balloons. They were regularly hit and were a spectacular sight as they sank, burning, to the ground.

We saw the puffs of smoke from the flak shells exploding high up amongst the clouds and heard the thudding of the anti-aircraft guns booming from a long way off along the coast.
The night raids were a lot more frightening, and although we were far enough inland to be relatively safe, a fleeing Luftwaffe pilot gave us first-hand experience of what it was like to be bombed. He jettisoned his last two bombs at our end of the village, one winter night, to fall in the fields close to Moorlands Road. The raid that night had been unusually noisy, and I had crept out from the bedroom, unable to sleep, to come out to the kitchen where my mother was making supper regardless for Dad. She was laying the table, and the kitchen was full of the smell of bacon frying, I remember, when we felt and heard the thump of a tremendous explosion. My mother and I fell to the floor as the house shook and the windows blew in, shredding the blinds. The ceiling came down, and covered the table and the food with dust and plaster. It was chaos. My father had been watching the raid from the back garden and had flung himself under the hedge. Shaken, he came inside, dusting himself off and told us how narrow our escape had been, as the plane had come right across our road, flying quite low and dropping bombs as he flew.

I have no recollection of air-raid wardens coming round, but I do remember we had to clear up the mess in the kitchen before we went to bed and get a blanket fitted up over the window as black-out!

The next morning—a Sunday—the field across from our bungalow, on the Bishops Waltham road, was packed with 'sightseers' as people from all around had come pushing through the hedge, to see our first bomb-crater. My father took us to see it, and it was truly impressive. It was very deep and wide, I remember, and about the size of two of our bungalows. It was indeed from a very large bomb. People wandered around the edge talking and staring—all the boys scrabbling down amongst the debris to collect what shrapnel they could find, for souvenirs! The farmer had to barricade the hole in the hedge after that to prevent hordes from coming to have a look!

The second bomb had actually fallen in the top end of his farmyard along the road, blowing a tree right out of the ground by its roots, and it hung for many months in the branches of another tree—referred by us children, from then on, as the upside-down tree!

Other raids did not come as close to the village, but they still had their terrible effect on our lives. One wet July or August afternoon in the holidays, we watched a particularly violent raid going on over towards Eastleigh, in the West. My mother's friend had been with us for the afternoon, having a cup of tea and gossiping in the front room, and we children had been left in the kitchen to play. Again, a fleeing plane had dropped bombs across the fields as we watched from the window—my brother Ken, aged six, shouted to us to look. The house shook, and we ran outside to see where the tell-tale smoke was—it was near the horizon, over towards Eastleigh, and there were clouds of smoke and dust filling the sky.

Our neighbour, Frederick Bath was one of those killed in the Cunliffe Owen factory (now Ford's) at Eastleigh, as was Frederick Willing, the son of the licensees at the Rising Sun.
Daylight raids on Portsmouth and Southampton became something of a regular spectacle, and by now we did not always stop our play to watch and wonder, unless things got too close or too noisy! However, one Spring evening was an exception.

A raid must have been going on while we were having our tea—bread and jam as usual—as immediately we had finished we all went out to the gate to get a better view of what was going on above us, in the skies over Southampton. It was daylight and still warm, and my brothers had run off to play with others in the road. It was a bonus to be allowed to stay up a little later and to play out after tea. We were usually packed off to bed before my father came home from the shop for his tea.

Other women had come to join to join us outside to watch the planes circling round each other in dog-fights, gun-puffs filling the sky. We were ready, of course, to take cover under the hedge should the fighting get too close. As usual, I stayed near to my mother, but I knew it was more exciting to be out in the road watching the raid than inside not knowing what was going on.

It had been a long and violent raid and we were expecting the 'all clear' at any time. The skies had cleared of planes and the sound of the gunfire had faded. White puffs of smoke from exploding shells had merged with the evening clouds. Suddenly, as we began to drift away, with mothers rounding up their children for bed, as if from nowhere, a blazing German plane came hurtling low through the air, with the cross mark clearly visible. It came from across the field at the end of the road. Everyone screamed and watched in terror as the blazing plane came towards us, lurching ever closer and falling all the time. It crossed above us and passed over the rooftops opposite towards the ridge of the downs at Dundridge, where it crash-landed in a field. As of one, all the older boys tore off in pursuit, up the road and across the top field. My brother, aged seven, ran with them, but soon got left behind. Some of the mothers walked to the top of the road to get first reports back, and eventually we all heard that the Civil Defence had arrived at the scene within minutes, and had cordoned off the whole area.

Smoke and dust were already visible over the trees as the 'all clear' sounded, but the excitement of the events remained in the air—we had never seen a German plane so near before and speculated over the fate of the pilot. We also knew that the plane could well have landed in our road! Was the pilot already dead or wounded? We will never know. Debris from the crashed plane was strewn over a large area and we were told there was a huge crater in the field where it landed.

Some weeks later we pushed my young sister Sheila in the pushchair along that top lane, to look at the scene of the crash, and I remember standing by the mangled hedge to look at the chalky white crater. For many years there was a distinct chalky scar in that field, even when it was ploughed, a white reminder of the young German pilot who died there.

Evacuees

Quite early on in the War, in the Spring of 1940, my mother was interviewed on the doorstep by an official-looking woman with a clipboard. Curious as ever, I gathered that we were being asked if we could take in evacuees from Gosport, as children were being evacuated from all areas where there was danger of bombing. My mother already had five children, so we were not allocated any, but many other households we knew were.

The evacuees arrived one Saturday afternoon at our end of the village. We stopped our play

36

in the front garden to peer over the fence at this noisy jeep-load of crying children. We saw two boys being escorted into the house next door, with their bags and suitcases. Fortunately, our mother had heard all the noise and took us indoors, away from the commotion.

However, from that day on our lives were changed out of all recognition. These street-wise children (the boys at least) did not cry for long, and during the following Summer months we spent all our daylight hours outside playing with them and following them around. They climbed telegraph poles, explored our fields and lanes, and climbed trees. They made dens and formed gangs and went for long walks across the Moors. I went with the "big girls" to pick primroses and violets and discovered a whole new world. The Moors are still wild, but in those days the stream of the River Hamble flowed deeply from the spring towards the Mill Pond at Waltham Chase, and we spent hours between the watercress and the kingcups paddling and making dams and bridges there.

Around the village these children ran and shouted with a wild energy that country children do not have, and they would not be called in for bed. They rode two to a bicycle and queued for chips at the new fish and chip shop in the village. With double Summer Time we all played out in the sunshine till late at night if our mothers could not find us! I remember those months and years as being nothing but glorious, with new exciting friends and the freedom to run wild across the fields.

Many of the evacuated children were homesick and suffered considerable problems in adjusting to rural life, with a large number returning home to their parents once the immediate danger from the Battle of Britain was over.

Some, however, did stay for the duration of the War and became part of the village. One of these was a boy called Norman, who lived with a neighbour in No. 5 Moorlands Road. He was about eight years old when he came—a fair, curly haired boy—and he quickly became friends with my middle brother, Doug. He spent a lot of time in our house playing with what toys we had, or out riding on our bicycles. I think his mother was busy working and felt he would be safer out in the countryside, and the woman who billeted him gave him a good home. He went back at the end of the War, and I often wonder if he ever came back to see anyone.

While the evacuees were with us, we had half-day schooling—the evacuees had the mornings and we had the afternoons. Various halls around the village we called into use—the British Legion Hall, the Reading Room and the Methodist Church Hall. It was all very novel, especially as strange teachers (married teachers, I suspect) from all over, were drafted in to teach us. To compensate, we had lessons in the holidays and I for one went to some of these.

My heroes for the next four years, however—twin boys from Yorkshire, Richard and John—were not strictly evacuees, as their mother had taken a job as a housekeeper to a retired Army Captain, along the main road. One Spring morning in 1942, they literally pole-vaulted over our fence and into my life! I had been playing dolls with an evacuee girl on our front lawn but these freckle-faced boys with their khaki shorts and northern accents were a far more interesting prospect. I chased them back off the lawn, time and time again, until Patricia ran crying to my mother, and that was that. We then had to play in the back garden!

The twins were initially allocated to my class at school and for the next few years they were my life. Surprisingly, I was allowed to roam everywhere with them, once my father had gone off to the War! My mother liked them as they were good to the younger children and they were always polite to her.

In those Summer months we followed the harvester round the cornfields and built stooks with the sheaves. We slid down the ricks after the threshing machine had gone and played tag round the stooks—and later on kiss chase and "Truth or dare". It was all very daring and exciting and totally innocent. We swam in the River Meon at Mislingford, jumping and diving off the waterfall, and often, if I was lucky, I had a ride home on the crossbar of one of their bicycles,.

As the years went by, though, the twins, now about 14 years old, did begin to spend more time with the older boys and I was left to catch what I could of their company. One of my last memories of them is from one Summer evening of 1945. I was sitting at the end of our road, not wanting to go in, when I heard the loud singing of boys' voices, coming along the road from Bishops Waltham. They were singing "Wheezy Anna" and "She'll be coming round the mountain when she comes" and it was truly magical to hear their voices in the dusk. They had all been to the flea-pit cinema and were walking home. I was in two minds whether to stay, but as they rounded the corner the twins ran and sat on the grassy bank beside me. The big boys soon called them away, but I knew I was still their sweetheart!

The Home Front—My Mother's War

As a family we were relatively lucky, in that my father was not called up until 1942, when he was 34 years old. This meant that for the first three years of the War he was around to do all the repairs to the house and to do the garden. His weekly wage as the manager of Lankaster and Crooks, a grocery store in Bishops Waltham, also meant that we had marginally more money with which to take advantage of the ration points and coupons that had been allocated to everyone. Ration books for food and clothing were issued very early in the War (Autumn 1939) and had to be collected from the Ministry of Food (MOF) Centre in The Institute in Bishops Waltham, opposite the old Mafeking Hero pub. Ration books had to be taken to the shops and coupons were either cut out or crossed off. Although I do not have the details of how much was allocated to each family or how often, I do know there never seemed to be enough money in our house for all our food and clothing needs. We rarely used our sweets allocation, I do know! As there were families in the village willing to buy coupons, we were sometimes sent to these better-off houses to sell them—one errand I did not enjoy.

After my father was sent away to the War, balancing the books became a much more serious matter for my mother. Her weekly pay from the Army was only £5 a week, collected from the Post Office, and this had to cover food, clothes, rent, fuel and all other household expenses. It was an almost impossible task with five young children to feed and clothe. Life seemed full of difficult choices for my mother to make, and usually the choice was to go without. When the wireless broke down in 1943 it did not get mended, and when windows were broken they were boarded up for weeks. Often we could not afford coal and so collected wood for the fire from the lanes and the moors in an old pram, and when the lawn mower seized up, we cut the front lawn with hand-shears, all of us taking turns on our hands and knees! Wallpaper was a thing of the past and walls were covered in a ghastly pink and yellow 'distemper'.

By 1944, however, everyone had to 'make do and mend'. When crockery got broken, it was replaced by thick white 'utility' china cups, and my brothers even had white enamel dinner plates for their meals, from the Army and Navy Stores, I believe. Toilet tissue was also a thing of the past, and like most others, we used squares of newspaper.

To be resourceful during those years was an absolute necessity if families wanted to keep some semblance of normality, and luckily my mother's years of working in 'service' before she got married, now stood her in good stead. It was her training as a cook and a seamstress that really got us through the War! With good food her priority, on a tight budget she nevertheless always provided us with memorable hot dinners—Irish stew made from rib-bones and vegetables, toad-in-the-hole, spam fritters and shepherds pie from the minced-up leftovers from the Sunday roast. We also always had a pudding after every meal and these were really special—rice and macaroni milk puddings, baked apples and apple fritters and bread and butter pudding. Meal times were an essential high point of the day—dinners always at 1 o'clock (12 o'clock on school days) and teatime at 5 o'clock. For tea we only ever had bread and butter (margarine!) and either jam or chocolate spread—both home-made, with a fruit cake for Sundays only. We had no supper that I remember, or not until near the end of the War, when I was older and up with my mother until her bedtime, when we would have a cup of tea!

All our fruit and vegetables were home-grown as, like all the houses in the village, our bungalow had a substantial garden, and in rotation there was enough to see us through the year—runner-beans were salted down in big pots, while Winter cabbage and kale and sprouts saw us thorough till Spring. Potatoes and onions were kept in sacks for the Winter and with careful management we rarely had to buy.

Strawberries and raspberries, all set by my father, were turned into jam, as were blackberries from the fields, and plums and damsons bought from houses in the village. It was my mother's aim to make 100 lbs of jam each year, 2 lbs. for every week, for all our tea times and for use in puddings. She was very proud of the shiny, full jam jars stacked away in the larder! I was often sent to choose the next one to open for our tea! We also had two apple trees in the garden and apples from these, with 'fallers' from baskets put outside peoples houses, were bottled with the rhubarb, in kilner jars, sealed tight in the gas-boiler. My mother, with a little help from us, kept the garden going after a fashion—we could not afford not to!

In the Summer and Autumn, my mother and other women from the village, went to pick strawberries and then potatoes at Mcfarlane's smallholding, Hampton Hill Farm. She would come back home exhausted, yet laughing and smiling as she recounted the laughs they had all had. For years after the War, my mother and her friends would chat about these times, when they met in the village shop.

My mother made most of our clothes, sewing and knitting in every spare moment—during tea breaks in the morning, and after dinner. Cardigans, jumpers, baby-clothes, hats and mittens, and even our vests appeared from her knitting needles. By the time I was nine years old I could knit reasonably well myself, and eventually took my turn to knit mittens and balaclava helmets, and even, one winter, a many-coloured scarf! I taught my brothers to knit, and it was very rewarding to sit around the fire and compare our achievements.

The Gillard family 1944 - June 11, Ken 9, Doug 8, Mick 6, Sheila 4.
They sent this photo to Dad in India.

Dresses and skirts were run up on the sewing machine, as were pretty dresses for my young sister Sheila, and trousers and shirts for my brothers. I remember well, one year, how smart they looked in a brown corduroy suit of trousers and jerkin with elastic waistbands, and how all of them were sent from classroom to classroom at school, to show them off! Material for all this sewing had to be bought either at Lang's drapery store in Bishops Waltham or even from the odd trip into Southampton, to St Mary's market. Other sources of material were the regular Jumble Sales held in the village, where there were huge queues to get in, to get the bargains. Old tweed skirts were a wonderful source of material for boys' trousers, I remember!

My mother was able to earn a little extra money from her dressmaking, and on many occasions I would come home from school to find the table still covered with yards of material and paper patterns, with her busy on the machine, trying to meet yet another deadline. She made wedding dresses and bridesmaids dresses and was always in demand for alterations.

Shoes were a more pressing problem, but in those days shoes were repaired time and time again by our local shoe menders—Jack Linter in the village or Hector Coombs in his hut at Waltham Chase. Shoes were also handed down from brother to brother, and mine from my cousins at Hamble. One year, my brothers were given black ankle boots from a school allocation—boots with metal protectors on their toes, that made wonderful sparks when the boots were scuffed! On another occasion I had a pair of Clarks sandals, a real luxury but also a sound investment as they could be handed down several times.

As well as all this, my mother also cleaned at the Vicarage once or twice a week, and our family was on a list to receive food parcels from Canada. By dint of all these extra earnings my mother was able to give us a few extra treats at Christmas—a stocking each, containing an apple or nuts and maybe also a book or a special cardigan or jumper. One year, my father made all the boys a set of wooden cars and lorries and painted a wooden board complete with road markings and a filling station! I had a new set of clothes for my doll. Christmas was always a special occasion despite the War.

Hard as those years were, they were more than compensated for us by my mother's indomitable spirit, refusing ever to admit defeat. To be sure she would exclaim to me not infrequently "It will be the Workhouse for us, girl, if things get any worse", although where the Workhouse was she never told me! I can't ever remember her being depressed or miserable, or if she was she never showed it to us.

My mother loved life and, despite the war, gave us as many treats and days out as she was able to on her limited resources—treats and days out that I know she enjoyed as much as us. One of her greatest loves was the cinema, and she knew all the names of the 'stars' of her day, Errol Flynn, Greta Garbo, and Clark Gable, as she had been an avid cinema-goer when she worked in Southampton before she got married. Our local cinema in Bishops Waltham was no more than a 'flea pit'—a converted Oddfellows Hall, but whole families would walk down on Saturday afternoons or in the holidays, to see the latest George Formby film or Abbott and Costello. We even saw Shirley Temple on one occasion! The cinema was hot and crowded and very noisy, but we loved it!

Again, when Spring sunshine beckoned, there were other treats for us. Shutting the kitchen door on all the chores after dinner, she would head off down across the fields to the moors, to pick primroses or bluebells in the time-honoured country fashion, with us running wild around her, all of us glad of a day's freedom away from the house. "The fairies will do the washing up," she would say with a laugh! We would collect watercress from the streams and blackberries and crab apples in season, and on dark Winter afternoons fill the old pram with wood from the lanes. In later years we would roam further afield up into the woods of Upper Swanmore, in search of the rare wild flowers that were to become her passion. With an old technical book on wild flowers, we would be set down to minutely search for these new, lesser-known flowers that grew in our countryside. They were then pressed in our old, enormous Bible and then put into scrapbooks with their names alongside ready to be taken into school for the competition! My mother's enthusiasm was indeed infectious, and for years after I would take home any unknown plant I came across in my walks around the countryside. We did not ever strictly have picnics, but in the hot Summers of the War we did all go down to Mislingford for the afternoon with a loaded pram, with other families, to swim and paddle and walk through the tunnels!

Social Life in the Village During the War

Looking back, it seems there was a thriving social life in the Village during the War—maybe there always was, as people didn't go far afield anyway, in those days, with no cars and no late bus service. Fundraising for the 'War Effort', I guess, was as good an excuse as any, for a bit of fun and a get-together.

I remember being taken to some of the regular 'socials' in the Parish Room, by a young neighbour of ours, Marie Trivett, when I was 10 or 11 years old. Her husband was away in the Air Force in Iceland, and she would get baby-sitters in, so that she could help at these does. These socials were my introduction to another world! It was indeed strange to see women that I knew from around the village, screaming and laughing, as they played musical parcel or musical knees! We were rightly banned from the floor while the dancing was on unless we were prepared to join in! It was mostly Old Tyme dancing, I remember—dances with lovely names like The Valeta and St. Bernard's Waltz, and even the Bradford Barn Dance where partners were passed on! There were refreshments and a raffle and then a walk back home in the dark past Donigers Dell, a very scary experience.

I also remember going to some of the village 'Concerts', also held in the Parish Room. There were rows and rows of old wooden chairs and we children had to sit in the front, almost under the Stage! The star of the Show was always a certain Mrs New, a widow, with her rendering of I'll Walk Beside You and Keep the Home Fires Burning in her best operatic voice. She wore a lovely blue dress and high-heeled shoes, and her voice filled the Hall. She was truly magnificent—far removed from the rather stout woman who rode around the village on her bicycle! I wonder now, was she an escapee from the bombs of Portsmouth and had she sung in musicals in the Kings Theatre there? She always had tremendous applause, but we children giggled with embarrassment at the extravagance of it all! She was accompanied on the piano by another glamorous woman, a Miss Phyllis Watson, who always wore a red outfit and a fox fur round her neck. Again, she was an accomplished pianist and always gave us a recital, as well as finishing the Concert with her rendering of all the latest war time songs, for a sing-song. The hall was always packed for these Saturday night concerts—a real chance to meet up with friends and to applaud all the local talent.

Towards the end of the War, a beautiful dark haired girl, Sheila Willing, a niece of 'Pop' and Edith Willing of the Rising Sun, organised some tap-dancing classes in the village. A host of us girls joined enthusiastically, and we were soon tap-tapping our way across the Parish Room floor, with the metal studs on our bright red shoes! Once one had the hang of tapping it was possible to 'tap' anywhere and everywhere, even in ordinary shoes. We wore red checked dresses, and with red bows in our hair we were the highlight of all the later concerts. I was never good enough to do a solo, but danced along in the chorus line! Sadly, once the War was over, Sheila moved away and the classes came to an end.

As well as concerts and socials, there seemed to be a never-ending round of children's parties, in the Winter. These were most often held in the bigger British Legion Hall, along New Road. The hall would be decorated with home-made paper streamers and there would be long trestle tables, the length of the room, laden with sandwiches and buns and maybe jelly and home-made cakes. There were also beakers of orange squash for us.

Tea was followed by rowdy games with prizes, once the tables had been cleared. As the afternoon wore on, the room became filled with dust and noise and it was hard to tell where one game ended and the next began, with children running around everywhere and sliding across the floor. It must have been a nightmare for the women organising it all! The parties often ended with a noisy and emotional sing-song, with us children singing along with gusto and Phyllis Watson on the piano. I remember loving all those songs—*Run Rabbit Run, You Are My Sunshine and, of course, Lili Marlene and There'll be Blue Birds Over the White Cliffs of Dover.* Our favourite was *She'll be Coming Round the Mountain when She Comes* and the big boys had many extra verses that they sang to it! (She'll be wearing pink pyjamas when she comes!)

Garden fêtes were the great occasions of the Summer calendar. The only one in Swanmore that I remember was the one held in the Vicarage garden, a long way up Vicarage Lane. We went as a family, three of us walking and the other two in the big pram, setting off in good time to get the bargains! There were the usual stalls—cakes, white elephant and jumble, and plants, and lots of competitions and races for the children. Sometimes there would be a play put on from the Sunday School. There was often a baby show, with a prize for the prettiest baby and one year an ankle competition, which my mother won! To enter, the women had to stand behind a sheet with just their ankles and feet showing, and bare-legged there was 'our mum' winning the prize, which she was almost too embarrassed to claim! A brass band always played during the afternoon—a time to stop running around and to sit and listen to the music. In lovely sunshine it seemed to put a real shine into the afternoon—apart from the wireless we heard no other music. As the afternoon wore on and the money spent, we children rolled down the banks unceremoniously and played 'he' round the stalls, until rounded up, untidy and covered in grass cuttings, for the long walk home, and tea!

There were lots of Whist Drives in the Village, I do know, but my mother was too exhausted with the five of us to look after, to ever go! She was not a social animal and only ever went to Mothers Union on a regular basis, when we were at school. She preferred to stay at home with us, knitting or making jam or playing card games with us after tea. A truly dedicated 'Mum'!

Convoys

In the early days of the War, convoys of army vehicles threaded their way through the village to new camps—I presume to avoid the main road. They consisted of all the vehicles needed for war—trucks, jeeps, gun-carriages. The convoys must have been a mile long on occasions.

As soon as we had wind of a convoy, we left our games and ran to the end of the road to watch and to wave at the soldiers and stick our thumbs up to them. Some soldiers threw badges to the boys, and these collections became treasured possessions. Some soldiers played mouth organs and sang as they sat in the back the trucks, almost giving the convoys a carnival atmosphere.

The biggest convoy event of the war, of course, was in the spring of 1944. A huge convoy of the usual lorries and armoured cars drove through the village one day, but instead of passing on through, came to a halt in the village itself. By the time we had come out of school, soldiers had pitched their tents on all the spare ground available—outside the Mid-Hants Store, in gardens going down the hill past the Bricklayer's Arms and on both corners of Lower Chase Road and Hampton Hill. It was strange and exciting. The soldiers did not talk to us much, but we were asked to run errands around the village for cigarettes and pop. The soldiers seemed very big and real in their khaki uniforms and big heavy boots. They were French Canadians and teased us by speaking in French. They stayed for almost a week, and parents no longer chided us for being late home from school. Instead, they seemed almost anxious to talk about the situation. I know now that they had a fair idea about the impending invasion, but they didn't speak of it to us.

They eventually struck camp and moved out of the village and on to Bere Forest along the Wickham Road where I believe they stayed until they embarked for Normandy. I know now that the Canadian division was in the British Second Army under General Dempsey in Operation JUNO, and that they established the first allied Beachhead on D-Day itself, June 6th. I like to think that our village was the last English village in which they slept before they sailed.

The Doodlebugs (V1 and V2 Flying Bombs)

Although the air force would attempt to shoot them down, it was inevitable given their speed that many would find their way through. The Germans had the theoretical capability to launch up to 200 rockets an hour[1], all of which could reach their targets in less than 20 minutes and with a target area as broad as the London-Bristol-Portsmouth triangle, Swanmore was well within the 'danger-zone'!

For the three months between June and September, we had to be prepared for a raid at any time and be ready to take cover however we could. At first, as the dug-out had fallen into disrepair, our cover was simply the mattress under my mother's double bed and then the large dining-room table where there was space for the whole family.

As the bombs approached, we were told to listen for the droning sound to stop, as that was

---

[1] Source: H.E.Bates: *Flying Bombs over England.*

the point at which the bomb would stop flying and would begin to fall to earth to explode. As it was our experience that these flying bombs arrived either under the cover of heavy cloud or at the dead of night, it was truly terrifying experience to sit for those moments of silence waiting for the bomb to land and wondering if it would fall on us. It was these moments of silence that terrified us the most, and although to my knowledge Swanmore did not suffer a direct hit, I can clearly recall sitting with my mother and my brother Mick in the front garden one afternoon, listening to the approaching drone and then the cut-out and scouring the skies for any sign of the bomb approaching. It landed somewhere away to the northwest.

The last time I can remember a 'flying bomb' attack was during a period of almost incessant alerts—we had all been awake for most of the night, sleeping under the dining-room table when we heard the unmistakable drone of an incoming rocket and then the silence that signified the end of its flight. Of course we all jumped up and ran to the window where my mother was already rolling up the blackout blinds and we heard an enormous thud and felt the ground shake. A huge column of smoke and dust rose in the distance from where the rocket had landed on the pig-farm in Curdridge Lane.

The 'all clear' was sounded shortly afterwards and I remember playing in the road having got ready and had breakfast exceptionally early that morning, in the dark dawn of 'double summer time'. We later heard reports of huge damage with tales of dead pigs being literally scattered around.

The End of the War: 1945

The ending of the War was long awaited from about the Christmas of 1944. I remember my mother and her friends talking about it all and saying it would not be long before Gerry was beaten. Little did we know how bitter those last few months would be. Despite our meagre income, my mother had continued to have a daily paper throughout the war—The Daily Express—and she would avidly read the latest bulletins. I was now almost 12 years old, and she would encourage me to read the latest pieces on the battles taking place in Germany.

Then came the pictures of the release of the camp at Belsen, and I was initially forbidden to look at them. Later, with more and more coverage of the horrors of the prison camps being revealed, we looked at them together and speculated on the prisoners' chances of recovery. Bad as the news of the War had been, I think my mother was incredibly shocked at the full horror of it all.

VE Day was really a damp squib for us children! The village pubs were overflowing with people celebrating and we rode around on our bicycles to see the bonfires but we were not encouraged to stay. I believe there was a party for us in the British Legion Hall, but I cannot really remember—maybe it was while my mother was in Hospital battling breast cancer. (We were for a while billeted out to various aunts for what seemed an eternity.)

The dropping of the atomic bomb in August, in the school holidays, and when I was back home, had more impact, as again I heard my mother and her friend talking about it with incredulity. They knew it meant the end of the War with Japan, but as my father was already being brought home it was all rather an anti-climax.

Financially, things took a turn for the better when my father returned from the War. He had been given compassionate leave to return after my mother's operation for breast cancer (which was perhaps attributable to the stresses of her wartime rôle), and returned in the middle of the night, in September. Turned out of my mother's bed to sleep on the sofa, it was my brief to tell my brothers the news when we woke in the morning. I remember we all crept in to have a look at him sleeping in my mother's bed—and being very surprised that he was not at all burnt brown from all that Indian and Burmese sun!

He went back to his old job at Lankaster and Crooks in Bishops Waltham, after only a few weeks leave. His 'gratuity' money was soon gone, however, on essentials such as a new bed for me, a new wireless, a new lawn mower and new curtain material to replace the black-out blinds.

However, adjustments had to be made in this post-war world. We had earlier bed-times, there was no more playing out in the fields till all hours, and my mother was no longer free to abandon the chores and skip off down the fields with us, leaving the washing-up to the 'fairies'. I went off to the Grammar School in Winchester, having passed the eleven-plus and came home laden with homework, and a changed view of society. I discovered there that many of the girls had not had the sort of war that I had had. Worst of all, my favourite evacuee friends, twin boys from Yorkshire, who had been my constant companions for almost four years were now spirited away with their mother, and I was left to mourn their loss.

In 1946 too, we had a new baby in the house. It was certainly all change. Life that had been on hold for almost six years now seemed to be streaming away in all directions. My mother, who lived a full and active life until she was nearly 80 years old, was truly one of the unsung heroines of the War.

Home Guard

First known as the Local Defence Volunteers (L.D.Vs), this great force of part-time soldiers, numbering over 1,500,000 men, was Britain's Citizen Army. Raised in May 1940, it was mainly intended to combat the possible activities of enemy parachute troops in the event of invasion, the threat of which then seemed imminent. Throughout the anxious summer and autumn months of that year, each unit of L.D.Vs kept watch and ward over its own locality, thus covering the length and breadth of Great Britain with a protective network of vigilant patrols. The L.D.Vs were affectionately known as the "Looked, Ducked and Vanished", although this very much undervalued the important role they undertook.

In August 1940 the name of the force was changed to the Home Guard, and its hitherto improvised organization was placed on an established basis. Sorely needed equipment slowly but surely began to reach its eager members, and a co-ordinated scheme of training was put into operation. By the end of the year, its personnel constituted 1,200 battalions, 5,000 companies (or 25,000 platoons), a large proportion of which was adequately armed and clothed in regulation serge battle-dress. Early in 1941, Home Guard officers were granted the King's commission, and non-commissioned ranks were adopted on the Army model.

The problem of providing effective training for hundreds of thousands of men in the restricted time available in their leisure hours, however gladly given, proved a difficult one. Of great value were the special schools of instruction established at first independently and later under War Office supervision, where officers and N.C.Os received intensive instruction in field training, which they subsequently imparted to their units. Cooperation with the Regular Army, developed on an increasing scale, was also an outstanding help to efficiency. After long and patient waiting the Home Guard was equipped with a variety of powerful arms, including grenades, automatic rifles, light and heavy machine-guns, mortars and anti-tank weapons, all of which they were well qualified to handle.

The Home Guard was unpaid, receiving only a nominal subsistence allowance when on long periods of duty. Its original terms of enrolment permitted resignation at a fortnight's notice and stipulated that members should not be required to leave their own localities. Early in 1942, however, drastic changes were made. After February 16th, no member could resign unless in exceptional circumstances, and power was given in event of invasion for units to be moved outside their own areas. A maximum training period of 48 hours per month was required, and the Home Guard became liable for Civil Defence duties.

Up to May 1942 the Home Guard as a whole had not been called upon to go into action, but during the months of heavy air bombardment in the autumn and winter of 1940 many units gave invaluable help to civil defence, and individual members were honoured by H.M. the King for their courage and devotion to duty while under fire.

On May 14, 1942, the Home Guard celebrated its second anniversary, and the King honoured it by becoming Colonel in Chief.

Book to Consult: Home Guard Warfare, J.Langdon Davies (Routledge).

With the Bishops Waltham and Swanmore Home Guard
by Ron Crook

I joined the Local Defence Volunteers (later called the Home Guard) at Bishop's Waltham in 1940, while I was working for the West Hants Electricity Company. The Commanding Officer was Major Gunner of Gunner's Bank; although we attended all the lectures, parades etc., we were excused guard duty because we were on call to repair damage to power systems during air raids.

At this stage, we were issued with the Canadian Ross 0.303 rifle (note that the rifles were always kept at home with the limited ammunition—ten rounds).

Ron Crook (picture from his Identity Card).

We had what was left of a platoon of Royal Engineers after Dunkirk, comprising some dozen troops, commanded by a young Lieutenant with two lorries, which were stationed in our yard. The Lieutenant gave lectures to the LDV/Home Guard, and also made up pipe grenades, comprising one-inch diameter water pipe, some six inches long filled with gelignite and scored with a pipe cutter and ignited with a slow match. He demonstrated these with some effect by us standing under our tin roof hut while he tossed a pipe on the roof. The result was shattering.

In those first days, apart from the Ross rifle, the platoon had one air-cooled Lewis gun with a rotating magazine donated by a retired Naval commander who had it on his mantelpiece as a World War I trophy. During lectures given by the Lieutenant Royal Engineers, on defending areas of Bishops Waltham, e.g., road blocks, the old soldiers from World War I said, (I quote),
"Sir if we placed a Vickers machine gun or Bren gun at point X, another at point Y and another at point Z, it would be well covered."

The Lieutenant, with an understanding but sad smile replied,
"Gentlemen, I agree with your appreciation, but the sad fact is there are none".

The drill hall was the "Elms Hut". This was on the opposite side of the road to the West Hants Electricity Company where I worked. There are two events that stand out. In Christmas 1940, there was a great party given by the Home Guard with the Royal Engineers invited with beer unlimited. It lasted all night – I suppose we all assumed that the invasion could be at any time. (Some time between the end of September and October we were in a local pub, and were all called out as it was reported that the church bells had been rung, but it was a false alarm and we, of course, were unaware that operation "Sealion" had been called off). The highlight of the party was pianist and raconteur, local tailor Bert Shorney. He made up the verses, highlighting the alleged dubious activities of some of the personalities of Bishops Waltham, of which Arthur Rooke, the local garage owner, was one (shades of the BBC entertainer of the time Norman Long—a song, a joke and a piano).

An event occurred in the Elms Hut during a training session (I was not present at the time)

Back row standing: Billy Harris, Ron Crook, Sgt. Maj. Jack Mills, Vic Trivett, Bill Saunders Front row sitting: Lt Centre, Lieut Green, Rt Centre Don Hibberd

when practising with the Blacker Bombard mortar. A range practice round was inserted and fired with disastrous results; the bomb disappeared through the closed doors and the mortar "legs" stood back on some unfortunate operators; however, only minor injuries were sustained.

I transferred to Swanmore Home Guard in April 1941 when I changed my job to work for Vosper Ltd, the builders of Motor Torpedo Boats at Portchester. The CO at Swanmore was Lt Fred Rudd (the local assistance officer) but not long after, he resigned and was replaced by Lt. Green. Our Sergeant Major and drill instructor was Jack Mills (late of Hampshire Regiment when it was blown up in Dublin circa 1922), one of the characters with a superb sense of humour; during a period of a gas scare, we were instructed to wear gas masks at all times. During one parade, Jack shouted, "GAS!" We all put on our masks except Harry Tibble (another character) because he had left his at home. Jack strolled down the line and, when he reached Harry, looked him up and down and said, "I suppose you are immune Harry".

We had a musketry instructor, Corporal Gadsby, a stockbroker and Captain in World War I. He instituted a musketry course and, if one passed to his strict satisfaction, he personally awarded a five-shilling piece. I eventually passed but, instead of keeping it, foolishly spent it on beer.

We carried out many mock battle exercises with neighbouring platoons and later with regular troops, both British and Empire. I recall one major exercise involving the Swanmore platoon in conjunction with others in the Meon Valley. Our patrols discovered that the regulars had "occupied Bishops Waltham" at night and were bedded down and were very tired. The exercise was due to start the following day, but the Swanmore platoon decided that the "War would start that night" (shades of the film "Oh What a Lovely War!" only in reverse). We managed to "capture" them all asleep including their CO. He was not at all happy and threatened to place Corporal Vic Page on a charge. He tried to bluster his way out of the situation and then to reach for his general alarm, but Vic having fixed his bayonet, suggested what he might do with it if he reached the alarm. It was the only time we won!

At the Rising Sun pub at Hill Pound, the landlord was a Mr Willing, another great character, who had just taken it over in the summer of 1940, and we were connecting the pub to the mains electricity (tragically that afternoon his son was killed in a raid on the Cunliffe Owen factory at Eastleigh—now Ford's). He came from London and became a member of the Home Guard. During the years from 1942, rationing in the South was very tight. Every time we went on an exercise with him, his wife packed a superb hamper.

Major Panton was a Regular and an Area Commander of the Home Guard who lived in Swanmore and was a regular visitor to our platoon. What we did not know was that he was a member of the secret Home Guard. He was very enthusiastic and he came on all our field and weekends under canvas. Come D Day, he tried to persuade the War Office to let him to take some of us younger members to the Normandy beaches to help unloading; of course no way were they going to agree. However, about a week later he did arrange a visit to Hardway, Gosport and we boarded landing craft with the troops embarked: also to Stokes Bay where the Canadians with their tanks milled around awaiting to embark. Not a sight one easily forgets.

As we attended public parades during the war, in conjunction with ARP services etc., Major Panton said that we should have a lance with a pennant and that Ron Crook being six-foot plus should carry it. The problem was the pennant; however my mother offered to make this. (Swanmore Platoon was part of the 30th Battalion Hampshire Regiment.) The Hampshire Rose presented no problem, but to put 30th Battalion on a pennant 16 inches by 9 was going to be difficult, so it was a yellow pennant Hampshire Rose in the top left hand corner but with three white Xs indicating 30th Battalion. However, because of a certain beer being advertised, the immediate comment was "We knew that the Home Guard liked their beer, but was there any need to advertise it?"

During the daylight raids by the Americans, one Sunday afternoon a B17 crashed on the Downs. Some of the platoon that were on exercise in the area guarded the plane. When I arrived, they were keeping anyone clear from exploding 0.5 ammunition.

Our firing range was at the Dean Farm, north of Bishops Waltham and for competition shooting we had access to the Army range at Chilcomb near Winchester. (Later in 1944, some of us became keen on shooting and fitted "Parker Hale" sights to our favourite rifle.) When we received the Sten Gun, we were issued with 9 mm ammunition that was captured from the Italians; however, this was unreliable and on occasions a round would "crawl" out of the barrel or stick half way with hair-raising results. I feel that that is why the Army refused to use this ammunition.

During 1942, we were issued with radios and I became part of a signals section under Sgt. Eddie Carpenter (he was the local wireless repair man). We were equipped with No 38 and No 19 tx/rx (transmitter/receivers). One day, using the No 38 for range control, I was in the butts and I lost contact; when I looked up I saw that most of my whip aerial was shot away.

Some of the more hairy moments involved priming and throwing the Mills grenade: our first instruction was given in the British Legion hut by a regular Army Sergeant—we were actually priming live grenades ready for Sunday throwing exercise. He made the point of how to squeeze the detonator and primer to ensure straight entry into the grenade, and not to scratch or heat the primer as it could cause a premature detonation. One only has to imagine how nervous we were. Throwing the grenades next morning was also a nerve-racking affair.

The schoolmaster, Mr Richardson, from Droxford was an expert in explosives. He used to remove tree stumps for the farmers near Botley using explosives. Because it was near opening time and the last stump was difficult he used a large explosive. A chunk of it landed on the Bugle Hotel roof, displacing tiles that dropped through the visiting general's soft-top Rolls Royce!

On to our guard duties at Hill Top, Upper Swanmore, the residence of our CO, Lt. Green. We did this night duty on a rota basis and slept in the barn. On occasions, Lt Green did a two-hour spell, but slept in the house. On this occasion he was to follow me, and gave me verbal instructions as to how to reach his bedroom. (Note that they were all sleeping on the ground floor and as it was a warm summer's night the French windows were open). When the time came to rouse him, I wandered through the bedrooms; I think that there were others sleeping there at the time, but in the semi-darkness feeling my way around and coming across what appeared to be a lady's nightdress I quickly retreated, so I never did wake him, and I did his two-hour duty. (I was a shy young man in those days.) I don't think he ever knew.

During the 1941 air raids, the RAF placed a power-operated neon light (normally used as a landing light) some 300 yards from Hill Top. They would start it up after nightfall and then depart until morning. At first we thought it was for guidance for our returning aircraft, but because it was red, we realised that it was part of a decoy system simulating fires.

During 1943 we were part of a Concert Party given in the British Legion Hall, in aid of Wartime Charities. The Home Guard played a scene of "before and after" (quite difficult). I was made up as the village dunce by the local waterworks engineer Bert Simpson. (Bert was an amateur dramatic entertainer specialising in Dickens characters; he sometimes played in the Portsmouth Coliseum Theatre.)

In 1944 I was billeted in the "Railway Inn" in Droxford (also known as the "Station Hotel", but now "The Hurdles") and I was on duty as the sergeant in charge of the Swanmore platoon to mount guard on the railway station prior to D-Day. I recall that there was a buzz that the Germans might try a parachute drop on various installations in Southern England. However, some two nights before D-Day, a large steam loco (I think it was a 4-4-0, but am not sure) pulled into the station. This was most unusual, as the Meon Valley line was single-track with passing places only.

That night the officer in charge was not from our local platoon, and when he arrived at the pub he said to me in a slightly hysterical tone,
   "There is a rumour that Churchill will be here tonight, and if you see him report to me
      immediately, but don't panic! (shades of Dad's Army!).

Needless to say we did not see Churchill, but he was on the train with Eisenhower, Montgomery, General Smuts and General de Gaulle.

However, early next morning I was on patrol inspecting the troops and across the field came two people out for a morning stroll. One of these was vaguely familiar. A man with a small pointed beard, and of course it was General Smuts. The other man was a tall, angular individual in a foreign uniform. As they drew closer I came to attention. Genera Smuts said, as I recall, something like, "Good morning, Sergeant, and this is General de Gaulle." General De Gaulle remained entirely aloof and said nothing, and they moved off in the direction of the train.

A few moments later, all hell broke loose! The Special Forces and Royal Marine Commandos

Private Alec French in the Home Guard. He was chauffeur to Major Portal.

who had been guarding the train were swarming around me in panic as they had "lost" two Generals. I reassured them that they'd returned to the train!

When we were on duty, Lt. Green would always come up for a chat, which invariably ended in a lively discussion way into the night. At one period, I think about early 1943, he promised that after the War ended he would take our section on a day and night out in London. Either late 1945 or early 1946, he was good to his word; I think there were eight of us, I remember Bill Harris, Reg Gray, Alec French and myself. We set off in two cars, saw a football match at Brentford, then on to a restaurant for a meal, finishing up at the London Palladium where Flanagan and Allen were starring.

At the end, at least Swanmore Home Guard survived without any injuries.

Swanmore Home Guard Stand-Down Parade 1944. Sgt Ron Crook is holding the lance with a pennant.

Memories of an Evacuee
by Ian Plowman

Although not a Swanmore villager, perhaps the memories of an evacuated schoolboy from Gosport will be acceptable and may add a little colour to the local history of the war-time period covering the early 1940s.

2 Cott Street c. 1959. The Plowman family lived here at the beginning of the war and they were succeeded by the Dodsworths.

Dad had the good fortune to find a safe refuge in Swanmore from the hostile air war over Gosport at number 2 Cott Street[2]. A charming thatched cottage complete with well, large cherry tree and a long history, which was part of the Portal Estate of Holywell.

Our arrival in the area as a family of three, was at the end of a long hot car journey from Sussex. Dad's first job was to start up the paraffin Primus stove with the idea of making a much-needed cup of tea. Where was the water supply? ... down the well of course!

Now, drawing water from a well by winch and bucket demands a lot of winding power and concentration not to let go of the handle when the full bucket nears the surface. This we achieved but unfastened the clip from the bucket handle. The inevitable happened of course and after emptying the bucket it toppled over and back down the shaft!

After that welcome cup of tea, Dad rigged a grappling hook and was fortunate to retrieve a bucket, but not the one we had lost. I suppose he recovered some ten relics

The Plowman family in the early 1940s. Ian and his father, Harry, are on the left; Ian's mother, Connie, is 4th from the left.

from the depths besides the one in question; several were in quite a sad state, having been down there a long time. Only recently I had been studying the first Ordnance Survey map of the area published in 1810 and a farm and cottages were shown then as Cock Street!

For a town lad, Swanmore and its farming community were rich in daily happenings that appealed to a schoolboy. The lack of public transport made the cycle a necessary link for keeping in touch. Mine came up from Gosport on the back of a Dyers Dairies milk-churn collecting truck, an ancient upright gents model donated by an uncle. It needed wood blocks on the pedals for me to reach the saddle.

Imagine, if you will, an eleven year old and total stranger to the art of 'push biking' setting off from the far end of Cott Street to get to the village school.

---

[2] When the Plowmans left Swanmore in 1941, June Dodsworth moved in to the house with her aunt. (See *Life in the Land Army* on page 54.)

During the first few days I needed the whole width of the lane, and occasionally the ditch, before any predictable arrival for lessons could be guaranteed. My journey would take me past the narrow cart track turning for Holywell, along a narrowing lane and through a tunnel of overhanging trees with a mysterious Tudor style cottage on the left; by Watson's Farm triangle and the Hunters Inn; across the main road and up the slope finally to the School opposite the Church.

I became part of an evacuee group that shared the School during the afternoons. Miss Austwick was the senior teacher; she owned a little Austin Ruby saloon, I recall.

Memories of that winter at school are still vivid after sixty years. Several of the lads decided the school playground would lend itself to an ice-slide. During lessons one morning, the usual excuse to 'leave the room' was achieved, and a hasty visit to the washroom enabled the use of the old steel mug that became mysteriously detached from its retaining chain. Numerous mugs full of water were splashed across the playground diagonally by a succession of boys. This froze instantly into a lengthy but efficient slide. It was ready by playtime and lethal, but we survived.

The snow that winter was quite deep in drifts around the cottage and we made good use of the field opposite to build ourselves an open-top igloo of sorts. The snow didn't appeal to Dad, though, as he was unable to negotiate the steep slope by St Clair's Farm when it turned to ice. It was quite a journey down to Priddy's Hard in Gosport where he worked as an armaments gunsmith; the road surfaces then were not of the present-day quality.

Because of Dad's peacetime job as a car mechanic, his knowledge was useful to Mr Smith when one of his tractors was giving trouble. He had two–an International and a Fordson. One used to start on petrol and could then be switched to run on paraffin.

That autumn had brought the usual crop of horse chestnuts to the trees by Hill Farm in Hillgrove Road. The road was much safer then for 'conkering'—a veritable gold mine that hardly needed any stick throwing. One just stood patiently underneath and the next gust of wind dropped them at your feet. I introduced our growing family to this spot years later in the 1960s, but the speed of vehicle traffic had made conkering quite dangerous by then.

Dad continued to travel daily to Gosport and his gunsmith's job in Priddy's Hard, having started there while we were in Billingshurst. A self-taught motor mechanic by trade, he was 'called up', being offered the choice of driving fire engines or working in armaments. He chose gunsmithing and was soon repairing Oerlikon, Pom-Poms, Bofors, Point-Fives and small arms, rifles and the like.

He would tell of families who trudged over the Hill from Portsmouth and slept rough among the trees that lined the main road by what is now the Roebuck Inn. Double summer time was observed then; it meant the working day lasted until quite late in the evening, getting dark around 11pm.

Mum and I soon found ourselves included in the help needed by Mr Smith, the farmer further along the lane, at potato harvest time. The 'spinner' would bring the crop to the surface and pickers would work their way over seemingly endless rows bent double. My attention span for this labour was quite short: next day I ached all over.

The potatoes were stored in a barn alongside the pair of cottages in Cott Street. Later they were 'riddled' in a hand-operated machine of horizontal wire trays that separated the crop into three different sizes. Woe betide anyone who left the door of the store shed open for the daylight to damage the crop. I believe most of them were bought by the proprietor of a Gosport fish and chip shop.

I was given a small supply of seed potatoes earlier in the spring and produced a surprisingly good harvest from a patch that I had dug over several times to make the soil suitable. My ongoing efforts as a 'townie gardener' were the subject of much comment. A young rabbit also expressed interest in the vegetation alongside my potato patch. Dad kept his BSA Air Rifle at the cottage and over several years I had been allowed to use it. It was a one-shot action and quite powerful. Dad had a treat of rabbit pie that evening, as Mum was quite skilled at skinning a rabbit.

Grain harvest time I liked, chasing the rabbits that scurried from the path of the reaping machine. This was a temperamental outfit where horizontal sweeping blades turned a circle brushing the standing wheat onto cutting blades and a conveyor belt. Mostly the problem was getting the binder to tie knots and drop the sheaves in an orderly manner. The sheaves were then 'stooked' in sixes and left to dry.

The threshing machine worked its way around the farms and was quite an event. I remember one warm sunny evening when I was included with friends of the Smith family and we rode to a distant field on a tractor-drawn trailer to lend support with the threshing. It was quite a jolly affair that included young lady friends of Mr Smith's sons.

Dried stooks were loaded at one end into the thresher. These were processed into chaff and straw for making the rick and finally pouring grain into a monster sack at the far end. A very noisy and dusty operation.

The Ministry of Ag' and Fish (Agriculture and Fisheries), in their wisdom, promoted silage production. This was supposed to be a simple process of gathering clover, tipping it into a large open prefabricated, asbestos-like tank and squirting diluted, sickly smelling molasses over each layer, thereby making cattle cake.

That was the theory! The squirting was done by stirrup pump from a bucket. Getting the dilution right to go through the pump was another matter. All the while, spray and leakage from the incarcerated clover stuck firmly to everything. It took days for the 'glue' to wash out of my clothes and the sickly smell to disappear. Mum was not happy. Even now the sight of a tin of Fowler's Black Treacle brings back the whole scene afresh.

Quite often I found my way to Holywell House to collect a daily can of milk from Sally, Major Portal's cook. This was a very pleasant duty because Sally made the most wonderful cakes and I suppose she had a soft spot for yours truly.

The path to Holywell was through the wood opposite Cott Street and led to the rear of the Big House and Sally's kitchen. By the kitchen door was a parrot in a cage that would announce my arrival. I had to walk past an aviary cage that housed what I can only describe as a large eagle-owl that I believe the Major had brought back from one of his travels. It never made a sound as I walked by, but would follow my progress with a foreboding hungry stare that was no doubt weighing up the prospect of a tasty snack. I loitered not at this point!

Before we came to live in Cott Street, Father had related the tale of the night he came close to being blown up by an enemy bomb.

Dad and his Grange Crescent neighbour, Sid Beaumont, used to sleep nights at Mrs Hebdidge's in Hillpound near 'The Rising Sun'. Aerial activity was very noisy at night over Gosport, so Dad and Sid (a gunnery officer at Whale Island) would retreat 'over the Hill' for a little peace and quiet. Dad kept his car in the barn of the smallholding opposite Mrs H's, that later became Meon Valley Vineyard.

He was checking that his valuable transport was safe this particular night when he spotted a strange hole alongside the barn wall. Further inspection by locals decided it was definitely alien, with all the hallmarks of a delayed action bomb. Nearby houses were hastily vacated and the landlord of 'The Hunters' gave them shelter for the night.

This was preceded by an agonising decision for Dad—should he leave the scene smartly and his car to its fate, or make a mad dash and rescue 'Lizzie' but risk being blown up? The car won and survived several years' safe motoring. The bomb exploded some unearthly hour the next morning and flattened the barn!

Another incident occurred after we had been living in the cottage for a while. I spent quite a lot of my time climbing the many trees that were close to the cottage. This particular afternoon I'd climbed a crab-apple tree in the field opposite and spotted an inviting looking hole close to the hedge below. Investigation aided by a long hazel pole that eventually slipped through my fingers and disappeared from sight. I mentioned the fact casually at tea and thought no more about it. The next day, I returned to the spot to find a whopping mound of earth—whatever it was, be it anti-aircraft shell or small bomb, it had exploded in my absence!

Dad made friends with a young family further along the lane by the name of Hurrell. Mr Hurrell was a musician on one of the Atlantic liners to New York. They decided an air-raid shelter would be a good idea and permission was given by Mr Smith to use the dell across the field from the farm and cottages.

This was the favourite haunt of local lads as it was a somewhat mysterious overgrown place carpeted with wild garlic that gave off quite a pong. Wild thick vines hung from trees that were ideal to swing from.

Mr Hurrell had quite a sophisticated affair prefabricated, which he dug into the slope of the dell. I recall it had a Dutch half-door arrangement. Ours was a less salubrious affair, Dad made a visit to the sawmill at Mislingford for supplies. It was not long after they had sustained a major fire at the wood yard.

We made use of our shelter a couple of times at night, but had to negotiate the pitch-black darkness across the edge of the field of peas to reach the dell.

My Great Aunt, a Mrs Flo Judd, owned a cottage in Holywell Road named 'Sunnyside', near to what is now Orchardlea. I believe she used to teach a Sunday School class in the nearby Chapel. Although a Gosportian, she spent some of her happiest days in Swanmore and it was her wish, when the time came, to rest finally in the Churchyard.

Two local folk from that time are especially remembered.

Sue Goater, a young lady in her twenties who lived with her mother in a cottage further along the Holywell Road. She was a delightful and capable girl. Liked by all and very adept in country life, she also drove a tractor for the Watsons.

Mr Tribbeck, the baker, on the corner of Chapel Road. He not only baked, but then found time to deliver bread and groceries and have a chat as well. I didn't appreciate then that Mr Tribbeck the baker was in fact the same Mr Tribbeck who delivered the bread to Cott Street until fifty odd years later when in conversation with Vera, his daughter.

It was a chance meeting that brought me into contact with Vera again. Not having had an involvement with the village since the war, and in response to a paragraph in The News requesting items for the Swanmore Millennium Exhibition, I related my war-time experiences as an evacuee in the village together with a couple of photographs. Being more than a little interested in calligraphy, I stopped by a table display of this ancient art only to discover that the calligrapher was Vera.

Sue Goater driving a Fordson tractor.

57

Barber, baker, mechanic all go back to the land

'Open air, regular meals made us healthy'

'A GRAND LIFE, FARMING'

Daily Express Staff Reporter
SWANMORE (Hants),
Wednesday.

MR. EDDIE WATSON stood on his 300-acre farm at Swanmore, Hants, this afternoon, tucked his thumbs inside his waistcoat, and said to me : "Yes, I must have the mo t versatile bunch of farm hands in the country."

His foreman is a qualified barber, his cowhand is an ex-builder and carpenter, the man who packs the produce for market was trained to be a baker, and his tractor driver was a garage mechanic.

Only one of these men—Percy Didymus, the foreman—chose farming as his career early in life. The other three all trained for something else, gave it up and went back to the land for their living. And when I spoke to them today not one had any regrets.

They told me how the open air, steady work and regular meals had improved their health. Not one wished to go back to his former job.

Instead of uncertain wages and poor food they now get a higher average rate of pay winter and summer, and a weekly grant of vegetables and milk.

Percy Didymus (right)—he cuts hair "as a sort of hobby"—talks with Farmer Watson. Small picture on the left shows Reg Harvey. He was once a baker, but says now : "Farming is the life for me."

Article on Eddie Watson's Farm in the Daily Express, 3rd Nov 1938.

Farming

An article in the Daily Express in November 1938 draws attention to the versatility of the workforce of Edwin Watson, the farmer at Hillgrove. Percy Didymus, his foreman, was a qualified barber, although he had worked in agriculture continuously, but Percy's three workmates, brothers Reg (Dink) Harvey and Ern Harvey, and Jim Parsons, had all trained in other jobs before settling for a

Molly Watson - John's sister - later Harvey.

Jack Hibdige with horses.

life in the open air. Reg (Dink) had started as a baker's apprentice on leaving
school. Ern, the cowman, was originally
a carpenter whose wages had fallen to as
little as 5 shillings [25p] a week in bad
weather. Jim Parsons gave up a job as a
garage mechanic in the Village Garage to
drive Edwin Watson's tractors. Their
wages on the farm brought in between £2
a week in winter and £2.10.0 [£2.50] in
summer. Another of Edwin's workers at
that time was 75-year-old Harry Cave
who had toiled at Hillgrove for 50 years but still reckoned he wouldn't swap occupations with
anyone!

John Watson, of Shapeton, whose father, Edgar, was
Edwin's cousin, remembers his Uncle Eddie as an
extremely efficient and meticulous farmer. Probably
as a result of forward planning, everything he undertook seemed to turn out well. Cornfields were
scythed around the perimeter by Percy Didymus
before the tractors dealt with the middle of the field,
and then once it was laid over evenly, other members
of the team gathered it up rapidly, took a few ears of
corn, straw and all, then tied them up into sheaves.
The sheaves were laid in groups of six, which formed
a shock. As the corn was normally cut before it was
ready, it matured in the sheaves, weather permitting.
In fact, oats were cut when the straw was relatively
green and the old saying was that oats needed four
bells in the field before they were picked up. Four
bells = four Sundays = four weeks.

*Scamp the terrier, who killed a record
180 rats in a day.*

During the war years farming became much more intensive as a result of the Ministry of
Agriculture Food and Fisheries' directives. Immediately prior to the war, between May and
September 1939, farmers were paid £2 per acre for grassland that was ploughed up in what
was known as 'the Battle for Wheat'. The aim was to have two million acres of grassland
ploughed in time for the 1940 harvest, and the target was reached in April 1940. To protect
the precious stocks of grain, the killing of rats was encouraged, the Parish Council offering a
penny for the tail of every one exterminated. Kathleen Hartley, Edwin's daughter who still
lives at Hillgrove with her husband Christopher, recalls one very proficient terrier, Scamp,
who at harvest time accounted for 180 tails in a single day.

Mechanisation gradually increased and for the male agricultural workers returning from the
armed services in 1945/46 there were considerable changes from old-time practices to absorb.

WOMEN'S
LAND
ARMY

Women's Land Army recruiting poster in World War II.

Women's Land Army

This organisation was designed to release able-bodied men for the fighting services. The W.L.A. was a section of the Ministry of Agriculture and was formed before the war. Lady Denman was the Honorary Director, and by 1942 there were over 21,000 volunteers on the land with ages ranging from 17 to 42.

Choice of work varied from tractor driving and dairying to forestry and market gardening.

The uniform consisted of corduroy breeches, green pullover, fawn shirt, brown felt hat, stockings, shoes, boots or gumboots, overall coat, dungarees and a warm overcoat.

Life in the Land Army
by June Churm (née Dodsworth)

I joined the Land Army during the early 1940s and had the good fortune to live with my Aunt Flo Dodsworth at No. 2 Cott Street, Swanmore, a thatched cottage on Major Portal's estate of Holywell. The cottage, a semi two-up-and-two-down, had no bathroom, or indoor toilet, so bath night meant lighting a fire under a 'copper' which was housed in the tin-roofed wash house in the garden – the water for your bath and laundry I think had to be from a well in the garden.

My Uncle Archie, Gamekeeper at Holywell, had his call-up papers at the same time as Tim Adams, Major Portal's Under Gardener, and Archie asked me if I would like to take Tim's job, as Major Portal was allowed to employ one Land Girl and my call-up papers were due, so it worked out very well.

At that time I was working as a hairdresser and manicurist at Havant, going into the air raid shelter with customers and I could not understand why because I was the one told to look out and see what was happening and seeing the Flying Fortresses overhead and the Spitfire's from Thorney Island and Tangmere aerodromes with them. The Forts looked enormous in those days. I was the youngest at the shop so my job, before the shop opened (which was the same in most shops then) was to sweep the pavement outside our shops.

I also had to shelter in a shop doorway one evening when the air raid warden walking up the street shouted to people to get off the street. A frightened shire horse had escaped from its field, galloped through Havant's main street followed by machine gun bullets from a German plane which was about to crash, the pilot trying to do as much damage as it could. The plane crashed on to the cricket pitch, the pride and joy of Stansted House, a (smallish) stately home north of Havant owned by Earl Bessborough. The pilot's boots were put on show outside Havant Police Station. A friend of one of the girls I worked with was shot when she was collecting her washing from her garden.

As we lived near Portsmouth, we spent a lot of nights in our shelter at the end of the garden, so the thought of a quiet time, I hoped, at Swanmore sounded perfect. One of my clients at the shop was the organizer for the recruitment of the Land Girls so before I had time to change my mind, my uniform (2 pairs of overalls, 1 pair of cord trousers, 2 blouses, 1 green pullover, 1 overcoat, 1 felt hat, 1 pair of shoes and 1 pair of boots) were packed and I arrived at Cott Street.

On my first morning, I cycled through the woods to the gardens, my hair in order, lipstick on and red nails perfectly groomed, to be greeted by Mr Gilbert, head and only gardener, three of the farm workers and a huge pile of hot steaming manure. I did realize they wanted to see my reaction. I was told where to spread it and got started, and after a few fork-fulls the novelty faded and the lookers-on went back to their work. When I arrived home that day the zinc bath was in front of the fire. Flo had filled the copper and boiled the water. We carried the pails of hot water into the house and I was told to get in and have a good soak and when I had dried myself, she rubbed me down with a foul smelling liniment. "If not", she said, "I would be so stiff the next day." I looked on the bottle label and saw it was for horses, so instead of smelling sweetly of our favourite perfume, "Evening in Paris", the next morning I smelt of something which certainly kept the insects away. After a while Mrs Portal let me have the use of the servants' bathroom. We always made sure the door was locked when we had our bath at Cott Street as there was no guarantee Mrs P or one of the neighbours would not tap on the door and come in.

On my second day at work Major Portal came to the garden early to see if I had settled in, gave me a pair of gardening gloves so that I didn't spoil my hands, he said, and gently explained I should have cleaned my forks and spades I had used the day before. "Clean tools make good workmen", he said.

I didn't do any manicures but worked up a good hairdressing round in Swanmore and Droxford. I gave Major P his haircuts and remember doing Mrs P's hair one Saturday morning as she was going to a wedding that afternoon. There had been an air raid somewhere the night before, which had affected the electrics, so she had to sit in front of the fire to dry it. Major P had a generator in the cellar in times of emergency but I'm not sure what happened to it on that day. Another of my customers was Mrs Warburton Lee; her husband, a Captain in the Navy had been killed when his ship was lost at the battle of Narvik[3]. I think he was awarded a V.C. I remember she had a large crest in the hall with the name of the ship and Narvik on it. I also did the hair of her friend who stayed with her sometimes – Peggy Ashcroft the actress, who later on became a Dame.

My job on a Thursday was to cycle to Swanmore to collect meat pies. Agriculture workers were allowed one pie a week. I think the pies were made by the W.I. and that Mrs Portal at that time was their President, as the spare fruit from the garden and orchards were taken to the village and the W.I. had a canning machine so they were kept busy feeding the nation.

Miss Parker was the housekeeper and cook for Mrs P. I watched her making the butter from the Jersey cows' milk. It was poured into a barrel on a frame and turned around until you could hear the bumps of the butter. A bung was taken out and the wey emptied out and saved for the piglets to drink. The butter was a lovely deep yellow and tasted delicious. No butter

---

[3] See the article on Captain Warburton-Lee VC on page 73.

Wedding of June Dodsworth to Bill Churm.

has ever tasted as good as that. I watched her serve up a pheasant to take to the dining room after placing the tail feathers back in to it, and a rabbit she had stuffed with herbs, etc. Its head had been left on and it had been placed on a serving dish in a standing position.

I remember a group of young Canadian soldiers walking through the field by the gardens, stopping and talking to me and having a smoke, (I did in those days) and saying they had a rest day. We heard some time later they had to go on the raid to Dieppe on the French coast; the news bulletin later mentioned heavy casualties.

My days when I worked outside the gardens made a change. When the potatoes in the field were ready for collecting, the horse and plough would dig them up and myself and three farm hands would collect them. The chap with the horse knew I didn't like the horse stopping by me but always it would be pulled up by me and when we had all finished for the day he told me to take the horse and cart back to the stables. I remember telling him I had never driven a horse anywhere so had no idea what to do. He said "You just hold the reigns loosely and the horse will take himself and you home. If he "passes wind" (my words, his was a bit more rustic— Walter Gabriel type in the Archers) it means he is running out of petrol".

I enjoyed my time in the Land Army. I spent most of the time working in the garden so had an easy time compared with lots of the L.A. girls, so I have happy memories.

P.S. I left to get married in 1943, and felt very honoured that Mrs P gave me her family veil to keep, as she had no family; I still have it wrapped in tissue as a memento.

(An anonymous poem written in tribute to the Land Girls during the Second World War.)

I saw a Land Girl working
Alone in an open field.
Her, hard once elegant, hands
A stalwart hoe did wield.
Her back was bent as she slew the weeds
That spoiled the potatoes' growth;
She never wilted, she never paused,
She had taken her silent oath.
At last the day was nearly done,
The sun was sinking low;
She gathered up her jacket
Then slowly cleaned her hoe

She passed the chair where I sat
(I am feeble in body and sight).
She smiled at me as she said
"Been hot to-day. Good-night."
We hear the valiant deeds of our men in
"furrin parts",
Deeds which bring the tears to our eyes, a
glow of pride to our heart-
But when the war is over and peace at last
restored,
I shall always remember the Land Girl, who
made her hoe her sword.

Voluntary Aid Detachments

In 1909 the War Office initiated the Scheme for the Organisation of Voluntary Aid, under which the British Red Cross Society was given the role of providing supplementary aid to the Territorial Forces Medical Service in the event of war. In order to provide trained personnel for this task, county branches of the British Red Cross Society organised units called Voluntary Aid Detachments. All Voluntary Aid Detachment members (who themselves came to be known simply as 'VADs') were trained in First Aid and Nursing, and within twelve months they numbered well over 6000.

Membership of the Detachments grew still further on the outbreak of war in 1914. The British Red Cross Society and the Order of St John of Jerusalem, a body which was also empowered to raise detachments under the War Office Voluntary Aid Scheme, combined to form the Joint War Committee in order to administer their wartime relief work with the greatest possible efficiency and economy, under

Jean Edney, VAD, born in Spring Lane in 1921. She served throughout the war, mainly at Netley Hospital, and often cycled to the hospital and back during the Southampton air raids.

the protection of the Red Cross emblem and name. This was such a successful working partnership that when World War II broke out in 1939, the British Red Cross and Order of St John joined together again to form the Joint War Organisation.

The Royal Victoria Hospital, Netley.

What Kind of Work Did VADs Do?

The VADs working under both the Joint War Committee and the Joint War Organisation performed a variety of duties. Both the Committee and the Organisation administered auxiliary hospitals and convalescent homes in Britain throughout the World Wars. Much of the VAD service was performed in these homes and hospitals, and consisted of general nursing duties and administering first aid. Qualified nurses were also employed to work in these establishments, whilst many VADs gave their service in Military Hospitals. In addition, clerical and kitchen duties were performed by VADs and, as many men were engaged in military service, women VADs took on roles such as ambulance drivers, civil defence workers and welfare officers. VADs were also sent abroad during both World Wars as the Committee and the Organisation operated Commissions overseas in countries such as France, Italy and Russia.

Joyce Edney, VAD, born in Spring Lane in 1918. She served throughout the war, first at Netley Hospital and then at other military hospitals and reception stations.

Information courtesy of the British Red Cross Society website.

A bomb disposal lorry.

Civil Defence

Under the Air Raid Precautions Act 1937, local authorities were authorised to organise a General Precautions Scheme so that the country could be well prepared in the event of any hostilities.

By December 1941 the number of Civil Defence workers had reached more than one million, excluding members of the National Fire Service, with voluntary workers, including many women, far outnumbering paid ones.

Under the National Service Bill of December 1941 it was enacted that men of 35 and over might apply for Civil Defence duties instead of service in the Armed Forces. By the end of 1941, all were being equipped with a smart blue battle-dress.

The premier Civil Defence units were the Air Raid Wardens, who needed to be brave people readily able to act either individually or as part of a team. Each local area was divided into sectors and posts, which were supervised by a Chief Warden.

Wardens' duties included the reporting of all incidents arising from hostilities, including the extent of air raid damage and locations of unexploded bombs. Also they had to assist the relevant Police and Fire Service units that were sent to deal with the particular emergency, and to render general assistance to the public at moments of crisis.

Marjorie Harding (née Adams) with the Bomb disposal team at Bucketts Farm.

Bomb disposal team at Bucketts Farm.

Bomb disposal team at Bucketts Farm.

A bomb disposal team at work.

Droxford, Bishops Waltham and Titchfield Reserve Fire Brigade. Reg (Dink) Harvey is first left on front row, Stan Law is first right front row, and Jim Parsons is fourth from left in middle row. (All three worked on Edwin Watson's Farm at Hill Grove.)

Three members of the Searchlight Battery team at Hospital Road, Shirrell Heath. Ern Roberts is on the left and Paddy Degan on the right.

Members of the Searchlight Battery team at Hospital Road, Shirrell Heath. They include Fred Watmore, Laurie Norbary, Harry Carter and Paddy Degan.

A.A. Anti-Aircraft and Searchlight Batteries

The searchlight situated north of Hospital Road in Shirrell Heath covered Swanmore, with A.A. gunfire being provided by the battery situated in Rookesbury Park. Home Guard Personnel in many cases manned the batteries from dawn to dusk, thus releasing a very useful number of trained infantryman for the Army.

69

Employment

As a result of the war effort, a number of employment opportunities arose within the village. Timothy Whites and Taylors moved their packaging and distribution operation out of Portsmouth, taking over Swanmore Park House. Several of their key staff, such as Mr Gunning, a chemist, occupied cottages on the estate; his daughter, Joan, joining the local Girl Guides. Among present-day villagers, Eileen (Ciss) Talman (née Searle) worked there for a period alongside Vi Searle (née Wilkinson), later to become her sister-in-law.

Village ladies who worked for Timothy Whites and Taylors in Swanmore House in World War II. On the back row, the third and fourth from the left are Alice White and Gwen Hobbs (née Kirby). Phyllis Kirby (née Steele) is two rows in front, 3rd from the left.

Village ladies who worked for Timothy Whites and Taylors in Swanmore House (visible in the background) in World War II.

70

Following her call up, Ciss later worked for Cooksons Hermitage (a small arms munitions factory) just over the parish boundary in Shirrell Heath. Gwen Wood (née Downer), whose father was the landlord at the New Inn, was another villager on the workforce of around 50.

In New Road on the present Cortursel premises, Airspeed worked under contract from the Air Ministry gluing the wings of Horsa gliders; the corrugated iron buildings remaining there in the early post-war period. Ron Crook, who lived in New Road at the time, recalls elderly neighbours helping out in this vital war work. The site had originally been occupied by one of Swanmore's brickyards.

RM Brickworks, which had functioned in Brickyard Road throughout the 1930s, was taken over shortly after the outbreak of war by the Admiralty as a Boom Defence Depot, and Gwen Hobbs (née Kirby) worked there alongside her father Alfred. Alfred, who had been a police detective inspector before running the Bricklayers Arms in the 1930s, became a sergeant in the Ministry of Defence police with responsibility for the security of the depot.

Snooks and Goddards, wholesale grocers, occupied the present Meon Valley Printers site in Church Road for their distribution purposes, having moved out of the nearby coastal cities.

Cookson Hermitage Small Arms Factory workers.
Back: Gwen Downer, Ted Pond, Jean Simpson, Ethel Beaton, Eve Rumble
Front: Gladys Kirby, May Searle, Reg Holloway, Marge Willing, J Brown, Hilda Gamblin, John Saunders

Naval depot - RM Brickworks - in Brickyard Road.

Naval depot - RM Brickworks - in Brickyard Road. MOD Sgt Alfred Kirby on the right.

Working on the construction of Airspeed trainer aircraft at Studwell Lodge Droxford (indoor squash court) Gwen Wood (née Downer) is in the centre at the back. Similar work on gluing the wings of Airspeed Horsa gliders took place at the Cortursel premises in New Road.
Photograph courtesy of Hampshire Record Office Ref 217M84/32.

The Women's Institute
Extracts from the W.I. Minute Book

Sept. 20th/39 Owing to the outbreak of War the Members' Meeting arranged for Sept 20 from 7 to 10 p.m. had been cancelled and an Emergency Meeting was arranged on same date at 2.30 p.m.

Mrs Portal presided and dealt very fully with Plans for War Time. Members fully agreed the Monthly Meetings should continue and that Evacuee mothers might attend the Meetings at 2d each, tea extra.
The Committee had suggested no programmes printed for 1940 and this was agreed.

Papers provided by Mrs Portal – the Hampshire Chronicle to be exact – were distributed as they contained an excellent article by Hampshire Co. Council on wartime cultivation of veg. garden.

Mr Penning very kindly weighed the potatoes grown for Hospital – the contents were as follows:

Mrs Wainwright 8lbs 8 ozs
Mrs Hill 8 lbs
Mrs Gilbert 7 lbs

Sept. 20th/39 Mrs Wainwright was also presented with a prize for best W.I. poem competition held in July.

It was decided the appeal for British Empire Cancer Campaign could not be organised during present War conditions.
Mrs Law appealed for names willing to offer Blood transfusion, and Mrs Gadsby for helpers for a Working Party – knitting and sewing.

Signed: 15 Oct 39

P. Ethel Portal

October 15th/39	The Monthly Meeting was held at the Parish Room on Wednesday, October 15th/39 at 2.30 p.m.
New Members membership	Mrs Portal presided and was supported by Mrs J.W. Clarke. Mrs Gadsby and Mrs Wadge were welcomed as new members and cards were already distributed to Mrs Light, Mrs Pook and Lady Rose. There were 36 members present.
Food Production	Mrs Portal stressed the urgent need for food gardening as a help to necessary food production and appealed to members to use their influence in this way and so Dig for Victory. No support was forthcoming for a Produce Sub-Committee, the members felt they must tactfully find out from their husbands if they might be allowed to help in the cultivation or tidying up of their gardens. It was hoped the men would ultimately join the Sub-Committee.
Manure	Mrs Portal very kindly offered 6lb bag of Nitrate of Chalk – at 8d to help members make the best use of garden rubbish as a manure substitute.
Rugs	Mrs Tudway gave a short demonstration on Rug making. Members were keenly interested and the names were taken for a Demonstration class on Nov 1st in the Parish Room from 2 to 4 p.m.
Apron Competition	Mrs Tudway also judged the April competition. Mrs Wainwright was 1st and Mrs Gilbert 2nd.
Refuse Collection	Mrs H Watson on behalf of the Parish Council appealed for two members to collect subscriptions towards the Refuse Collection. Mrs Whitbourne and Mrs Light volunteered to help.
Rule Britannia Tableau	Mrs Strick, Mrs Light, with Mrs A Horner at the piano, arranged a pleasing Rule Britannia Tableau supported by Colonial representatives. The children were applauded and everyone voted the effort a great success.
Earl Haig's Fund	The following were willing to sell Poppies for Earl Haig's Fund: Mrs J.W. Clarke, Mrs Gadsby, Mrs Portal, Mrs Light, Mrs Smith, Mrs Strick, Miss Tier and Mrs Wellstead.

Signed: *P. Ethne Portal*   15 Nov. 39

Warship Week Carnival 1942 - the Women's Institute entry.

Swanmore W.I. Annual Report 1943

79 Members have paid a subscription during 1943, including 19 new members. This compares with a membership last year of 70 of whom only 7 were new members. On the face of it this looks quite good, but figures can be misleading. For instance of the 70 members in 1942 10 did not renew their subscription in 1943, so that although we had 19 new members our net gain in membership is only 9, and during this year 5 members have left the village.

Considering all the difficulties of the times the attendance at the Monthly Meetings has been fairly good, averaging just under half of the total membership. The Cttee. Attendance has been better, averaging just over three-quarters of the total membership.

Our Programme has been carried out without alteration, someting (sic) of an achievement in Wartime. Competitions have not been very well patronised, but the most popular were the Supper Dish and the Buttonhole done at the meeting.

Demonstrations at the Institute have included ones on Cookery, Make-do-and-Mend and Household Jobbery.

Talks have ranged from such a homely subject as Care of the Feet to Child Psychology and the United States of America.

Members have been able to attend Schools or Classes arranged by the County Federation on Thrift Craft, Clothes Renovation, Jam Making and Bottling, Pruning, Choral Conducting and Drama.

We have also been able to buy Seeds and Fruit Bushes for our gardens at special prices as well as Fruit Bottling Equipment.

During this year Work for the Community by Members has taken the form of organising and carrying out the Meat Pie Scheme, the Preservation Centre, the Rose Hip Collection, The Red Cross and St John Book Collection, and War Savings Group. Flag Days staffed by Institute Members raised £32-3-2.

Produce Guild Members organised a successful Garden Produce Show in July, cooked dishes for Potato Produce Week in Winchester during April, as well as Window Displays of Cooked Food at Fareham and Wickham.

The Drama Group acted the play "Some Person Unknown" at the Drama Festival in the Legion last March. They have suffered a great loss by the departure of their producer Mrs Geidt to London.

The Choir has practised throughout the year and took part in the Musical Afternoon at Fareham in November.

Our Delegate attended the Annual and Half-Yearly Council Meetings of the County Federation at Winchester in May and October, and we were represented at the National

The cast of the Women's Institute production of the musical, The Lost Heir, in the 1940s.

Back: Mrs Vincent, Mrs Boswell, Mrs Tribbeck, Mrs Gadsby, Miss Sheila Brooks (later Gunner), Mrs Draper, Mrs Horner, Mrs Carter, Mrs Stubbington, Mrs Thackeray, Mrs Hatch, Mr Hartnell (conductor)Middle: Mrs Doyle, Mrs Roberts, Miss Florence ?, Miss Wootten Front: Mrs Geidt (producer)

Federation Annual General Meeting by Shedfield W.I.

We have also taken part in all the activities of the Bishops' Waltham Group and have been lucky enough to have 2 of the Meetings, the Summer Meeting and the Musical Afternoon, held in Swanmore.

The Institute took part in the Letter Competition on Village Life, Past Present & Future coming out 15th out of 85 entries.

January 1944

P. Esther Pirlae

Swanmore W.I. Annual Report 1944

The 23rd year of our Institute ends with a Membership of 82, a very slight increase on last year. 15 New Members joined during the year.

The attendance at Monthly Meetings has been smaller than last year, averaging just over 32 per Meeting. This is at first sight disappointing, but an examination of the attendance register shows that in most cases non-attendance has been due either to illness or to the performance of some kind of war work. We are grateful to those Members who continue to pay their subscriptions although they know they cannot at present join in our Meetings.

Committee attendance is also down on last year, averaging just over 9 per Meeting.

Our Programme has been carried out with only three alterations, quite an achievement considering how much this area was in the picture on "D" Day! We have heard some excellent Talks, notably those on Moral Health, Local Government and the Work of the Red Cross for our Prisoners of War. We also had a Debate on the new Education Act, and a Demonstration of Cookery by Members. The most popular Competitions have been those done at the Meeting, and this fact has been noted by the Programme Sub-Cttee. in arranging the Competitions for next year.

Members have had the opportunity to attend Schools teaching Clothes Renovations and Slipper Making organised by the County Handicraft Sub-Cttee., and there have been special Schools for W.I. Officers and Members and for the Social Half Hour.

We have also been able to obtain Vegetable Seeds, Fruit Bottling Equipment and Leather Make-do-and-Mend Patches at special rates from the County Federation.

During this year Work for the Community by Members has included making a survey of local Water and Sewerage conditions at the request of the National Federation, organising and running a Fruit Preservation Centre, which made 355 lbs. of preserves for the Jam Ration, running the Meat Pie Scheme and a War Savings Group and Knitting for Liberated Europe. We all have the honour of being the first Institute in this Rural District to approach the Local Council to obtain representation for women on the Council's Health and Housing Sub-Cttee.dealing with Post-War Rural Housing. Three of our Members have seats on the Parish Council.

The Spring Council Meeting of the County Federation was cancelled owing to the Police restrictions on travel, but our Delegate attended the Autumn Council Meeting at Winchester in October and her report was read at the November Meeting. We were also represented at the two Business Meetings of the Bishop's Waltham Group, and nine Members went to the Autumn Group Meeting last month at Wickham.

Members have raised the sum of £10-9-8 by various efforts for W.I. Funds, and £14 was raised for the Village Forces Fund as the result of the Novel Raffle Table held in November.

The Choir, though much reduced in numbers, has carried on manfully. They took part in the Group Singing Afternoon in September, and the Musical Afternoon conducted by Mrs Rigg in November. The Institute was responsible for introducing the Osiris Repertory Company to Swanmore, who gave a splendid performance of Shaw's "Arms and the Man" last month.

Signed: C. Ethel Portal
(President)
17-1-45

Swanmore Scouts Remembrance Day Parade November 12th 1939

Swanmore Scouts and Cubs at Church Parade on 12th November 1939, in Swanmore (New Road).

*Group picture of the Swanmore Scouts and Cubs after the Church Parade
on 12th November 1939 in Swanmore.*

Swanmore Scouts

The 1st Swanmore Scouts kept a log book very meticulously from 1938 throughout the 2nd World War. It records their meetings and camps, and includes photographs and cuttings of the various activities. The tone expressed is often one of questioning whether they are living up to the high ideals of the scouting movement, as in the following extract, which was the first entry following the outbreak of war.

"WAR. September 1939 The amount of National Service which Scouts under sixteen can do in a rural district is so extremely small as to make some people think that we are not doing all we can. Actually during September we were able to give some small assistance to the evacuated children and to the billeting officers in their job of distributing the children to their new temporary homes.

The children are all under Scout age but we have a few visitors from Gosport (where the children come from) to our cub pack.

A few of the Scouts are attending weekly First Aid lectures and should become proficient. We have succeeded in Blacking out our own small hut and have been holding meetings there until the Parish room is also blacked out. This is being done by the Girl Guides.

Spent a lot of time in our September meetings playing football on the school field."

During all this time the skipper was not quite certain how long he would be in the district so P.Ls [patrol leaders]. are being trained to run meetings on their own. He is quite confident that they will be able to do it with flying colours if necessary.
However we shall be lucky to have the services of Mr Perryman, and when possible he will be present at meetings.
The book records the departure of J.H. Clutterbuck[4], the Group Scoutmaster (GSM) or 'Skipper' as he was affectionately known, on December 24th, 1939 when he departed for active service in the Royal Navy. There are pictures of some of the ships in which he served including the HMS Matabele. In his stead, Mr H.V. Perryman (mentioned in the above extract) took over the role of Scoutmaster, remaining in that position for the rest of the war.
During Summer 1940, attendances were small, as most of the boys were helping with the harvest. By December, owing to the severe air raids in Southampton, many men, women and children were seeking refuge in the village, and the Scout HQ was among the buildings requisitioned for much of that month.
The entry for the 30th December states, "Very small parade indeed, only 5 boys arrived at H.Q. It looks bad, such a small number, but people don't know what it is like when there is an air raid on. I don't think it is the boys so much – it is their parents as they will not let them out at night. That is the end of another year!!"

---

4. J H Clutterbuck had re-started the troop in 1937 after a one-year gap following the death of Mr Gladstone in 1933 and then his sister in 1936 They had taken on the leadership when Ernest Targett died in World War I.

In 1941 numbers increased initially but by late spring it is recorded that again attendances were very low as many of the boys were helping their fathers in the garden or on the farms. Monday meetings in early 1942 were devoted to the collection of waste paper and by March there were four patrols consisting of the following boys:

Foxes	Owls	Swans	Hawks
Mathieson P/L	E Houghton P/L	Roy Gibson P/L	Watson P/L
Ron Gibson (Sec)	G Crouch (Sec)	R Crouch (Sec)	P Parsons (Sec)
F Brewster	Kerley	Snook	Jacobs
Gordon Farr	C Parsons	Frampton	P Marsh
Parker	J Carpenter	French	

For the remainder of the war, numbers attending fluctuated between 4 and 24, and scouting activity was largely suspended during the summer months as troop members continued to help with the harvest.

It may be of interest to note that the Log Book does not even mention the end of the war!

Swanmore Guides and Brownies

Unfortunately there are no surviving log books for the Guides and Brownies covering the time period but it would seem that activity levels were fairly restricted.
Salvage collecting became a weekly occupation and there was a special Guides War Service Badge for this and other useful tasks, such as gathering rose hips.

Wartime leaders of the Swanmore Guides were Mrs Genevieve Doyle and, for the Brownies, Mrs Lena Watson, mother of John of Shapeton, together with his sister, Joan Watson, who was Brown Owl at the outbreak of war, before joining the WRNS and doing foreign service.

Guide camp at Preston Candover, VJ Day 1945, the first camp since 1938.
2nd from left is Joan Gunning, daughter of a chemist at Timothy Whites, Swanmore Park.

An ambulance for HMS Collingwood at Uplands House, Fareham, circa 1940, and a group of Fareham District Guides and Brownies (probably including some from Swanmore) who had raised funds for the vehicle. Far left is Muriel Wyatt, Fareham District Commissioner, who became International Red Cross advisor at their London headquarters.

The Dieppe Raid in August 1942

The Dieppe raid was acknowledged as a military disaster, although Lord Louis Mountbatten, Chief of Combined Operations, maintained many years later that for every one man killed on the raid at least ten had their lives spared on the Normandy beaches in 1944. Land girl June Churm (née Dodsworth) remembers encountering some of the French Canadian troops near the walled gardens at Holywell shortly before their embarkation in August 1942.

At Dieppe, from a force of fewer than 5,000 men engaged for only nine hours, the Canadian army lost more prisoners than in the whole eleven months of the North West European campaign or the twenty months during which they fought in Italy. Sadder still

A Canadian tank at Headley, near Bordon, Hampshire.

was the list of fatalities: 56 officers and 851 other ranks, which with casualties aggregated 3,369 personnel. The Canadians had earlier trained at Headley, near Bordon. Later the Germans, glorying in their success, dropped leaflets on the Downs near Swanmore, and Ron French of Mislingford was one of the local schoolchildren sent out to gather and destroy this propaganda. It seems at least one found its way into his back pocket, and it is reproduced here.

Canadian troops at Headley, near Bordon, Hampshire.

German Propaganda leaflet on the Dieppe raid - side l.

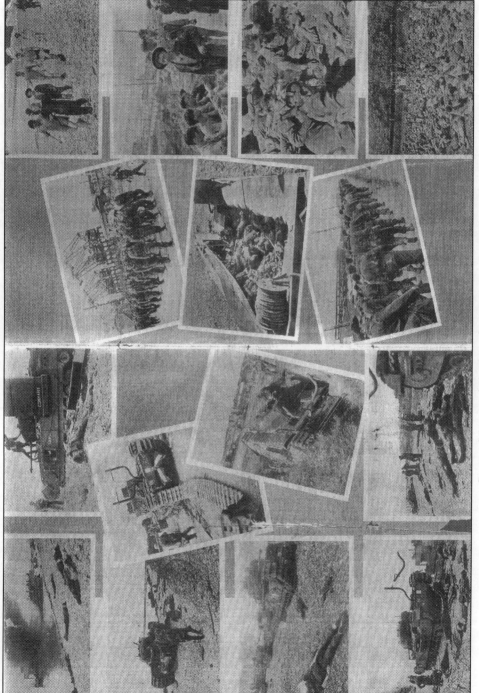

German Propaganda leaflet on the Dieppe raid - side 2..

D-Day – 6th June 1944

Nearby Droxford played an important strategic role in the planning of D-Day, and the famous 24-hour postponement was actually decided on a special Royal train kept in a siding at the village station. The train of eight coaches had arrived without even the railway staff being aware of the events about to unfold. A restaurant car with a top chef from Euston was an additional facility, as well as much up-to-date wireless equipment. In addition to Sir Winston Churchill, the world leaders who contributed to this historic moment were General Dwight Eisenhower (US military leader), Mr Mackenzie King (Canadian Prime Minister), General Charles de Gaulle (Leader of the Free French Forces) and General Smuts (the South African Leader). In the early days of June 1944, members of the Swanmore Home Guard platoon helped to provide surveillance for these world-famous personages as they reached their final deliberations, sometimes whilst strolling in the fields of our own lovely Meon Valley.In the

D-Day train - war leaders at Droxford Station. Mackenzie King (Canadian Prime Minister), Winston Churchill (British Prime Minister), Peter Fraser (New Zealand Prime Minister), General Dwight Eisenhower (US military leader), Sir Godfrey Huggins (representing Southern Rhodesia) and General Smuts (the South African Leader) Photograph: Hampshire Record Office Ref: 217M84/7

build up to D-Day, the shady lanes around Droxford and Swanmore were filled with tanks, lorries, and other armoured vehicles, all covered by camouflage netting and closely guarded by military personnel, including local Home Guard units.

Photograph: Hampshire Record Office Ref: 217M84/32

Droxford Station (for Hambledon), with a passenger train arriving.
Photograph: courtesy of The Stephenson Locomotive Society Collection

The Meon Valley Railway

The 22-mile Meon Valley railway line, linking Alton to Fareham, had its finest hours in the lead up to D Day on 6th June 1944.

Constructed in the early 1900s at a cost of £400,000 (the 600 labourers worked for 6d an hour), the line opened in 1903. The last passenger trains ran on 5th February 1955, although goods working between Droxford and Fareham continued till 1962.

There were two tunnels, one viaduct, 32 public road bridges, 12 cattle creeps and three river bridges. The five stations all had 600 ft long platforms, which were sufficient for main line trains, as the original intention had been to link London (Waterloo) with Gosport. However the advent of the motorcar in the 1920s and 1930s meant that the route through sparsely populated countryside never really became viable.

Today long stretches of the track bed are used as an official bridleway, and much of the original infrastructure remains intact. (The full story of the line is told and illustrated in *The Meon Valley Railway, by R A Stone.*)

H M S Duncton

During the war the village, in common with many others, 'Sponsored a Warship' and in Swanmore's case it was HMS Duncton. The HMS Duncton T220 was an Admiralty-built deep-sea trawler, coal burning, adapted for anti-submarine duties with all the appropriate weaponry and a top speed of 13 knots.

Vic Feltham pictured as a young crew member, who joined HMS Duncton in 1944, recollects receiving items such as hand-knitted socks, gloves, balaclavas and sweaters, although at that stage he was not really aware of their place of origin. During Vic's time aboard they were initially spending much of their time in perilous U-boat infected waters off the West African coast.

Vic Feltham, who served on HMS Duncton.

He remembers that one Cape Town trip was for refit and to be fumigated, as the ship at this point had become overrun by rats! The crew were billeted in Park Royal Hotel in Muyenberg where they lived a life of luxury! The food was brilliant, they had a bar on the ground floor and they used to go horse riding on the beach. When the money ran out they would play games of Monopoly in the evening. One game could last for several days!

After the refit they were sent out of Cape Town for sea trials. This exercise involved letting off a few depth charges. However, they sprung a couple of plates when they couldn't get away quick enough, so it was back to Cape Town for repairs! After being patched up they eventually headed back to Freetown.

En route to Freetown there was another unlucky episode when their engines broke down due to leaks in the boiler tubes. They were adrift in the Atlantic for a total of 21 days while dealing with the problem.

The following passages from the book *Trawlers Go to War* (*Lund & Ludlam, Foulsham, 1971*), has a reference to this incident. Duncton's 'Number One', Lieutenant Arthur Miles, recalls:

"A few days out of Walvis Bay, where we were called for repairs to our wireless transmitter, the engines were stopped owing to leaking boiler tubes. Spare tubes were fitted but more leaks developed. Our transmitter remained out of order so we couldn't call for help.... Fortunately the weather was perfect, whales and sharks playing around in the sea. One evening a sing-song on deck came to an abrupt ending when the lookout saw mysterious green flares, and Action Stations was sounded. Nothing happened and we felt like sitting ducks.... Food and water were now rationed, no fresh water at all for washing and everyone grew beards. Somebody joked, "Why don't we sail her?" and very soon this idea was taken

HMS Duncton moored at Devonport, just below Saltash Bridge.

seriously. The big foredeck awning made a good mainsail, and every piece of canvas aboard, together with some pretty odd bits of bunting, was hoisted up until the ship was festooned with 'sails'... There was a steady wind on the beam and the quartermaster steered from an auxiliary wheel aft ...."

"Every day our dingy put off on a practice cruise in preparation for sending a volunteer crew hundreds of miles north to the Portuguese island of Sao Tome to fetch help. This would have been very much a last resort, and luckily the most they ever did was take snapshots of us – the last sailing man-o-war."

"Fortunately we made one more attempt to get underway and eventually we were able to complete our trip back to Lagos. It was learnt later that next of kin cards had already been taken out at the base – we were very much back from the dead."

In Swanmore meanwhile, a plaque designed by Ettie Milligan entitled 'HMS Duncton' had been hung up in the Parish Room to remind villagers of the link. The plaque remained in situ for many years after the war.

Captain Warburton-Lee VC

Capt Bernard Armitage Warburton-Lee, who lived with his wife, Elizabeth, at Soberton Mill[5], had served in destroyers for 32 years when he was awarded the first Victoria Cross of the Second World War for his heroic action at Narvik.

Bernard Armitage Warburton-Lee VC.

The Germans having landed troops and sent warships into the long fjord on which Narvik lies, the Admiralty sent word of what had happened to Capt Warburton-Lee, who, with his flag on HMS Hardy, was patrolling at the mouth of West Fjord with four other destroyers. Reporting to Whitehall that the German force was bigger than suspected, he added that all the same he intended to attack at dawn. The Admiralty wirelessed at 1 A.M. the next day (April 10th, 1940) that they considered his proposed action so hazardous that he must be the sole judge of whether to attack or not, but that whatever happened they would support him. His reply was laconic – "Going into action".

With snow falling, so that the sides of the two-mile long fjord were invisible from his bridge, he led his little flotilla in. Reaching the bay in which Narvik lies, he signalled the other ships to patrol outside while he swept into the harbour at 20 knots to find it filled with German vessels. He promptly turned to port and fired torpedoes at a large German destroyer. His manoeuvre brought into view two more destroyers, at which he launched more torpedoes, and ordered his 4·7 guns to fire. The fire was returned with vigour, and, the heavy shore batteries having joined in and the Hardy having fired her torpedoes, Capt Warburton-Lee withdrew outside the harbour to enable his other destroyers to enter. When these had wreaked havoc with shell and torpedo, he took the Hardy in a second time, attacking the shore batteries. As he sailed out again, six torpedoes passed close to his ship, but the enemy fire had slackened. However, he decided to steam in a third time, but as he did so he sighted

---

[5] Soberton Mill had a Swanmore postal address, and by 1945 its residents were on the Swanmore Electoral Register. However the Warburton-Lees had strong links with Newtown, where they were benefactors of the village's Rookesbury Hall.

The name of Capt Bernard Warburton-Lee VC appears on the lychgate of Holy Trinity, Newtown, alongside those of other villagers killed in the two world wars.

HMS Hardy, 21st January 1937.

Dame Peggy Ashcroft in later life.

three large German destroyers coming out against him. A terrific running combat ensued. The Hardy was soon hit, but continued to fire back from all her guns until a shell burst on her bridge, reducing it to a shambles. The captain was wounded in the face and thrown on to the deck below. Another shell burst in the engine-room and it became obvious that the Hardy was doomed. Though mortally wounded, Capt Warburton-Lee determined at least to save the lives of his gallant men, so the Hardy was beached and the last order from his lips was "Abandon ship. Every man for himself – and Good Luck". His final signal to his consorts was "Continue to engage the enemy".

The Paymaster, Lt Geoffrey Stanning, later to become a Churchwarden at St Barnabas, had courageously steered the ship into shallow water in spite of fierce enemy attacks and grounded the HMS Hardy on the rocks.

Mr McCracken, the gunner, and a rating lashed their captain to a stretcher, which they lowered into the icy waters and slowly towed to the shore. When they reached it, he was dead, at the age of 44.

His Victoria Cross citation read, "For gallantry, enterprise and daring in command of the First Battle of Narvik, 10 April 1940".

In the wartime years the famous actress, Peggy Ashcroft, later a Dame, who died in 1991, was a regular visitor to Soberton Mill.
After the war his wife, Elizabeth, resided at Cringletie, Peeblesshire, but by 1966 she was back at Soberton Mill, and did public work in the villages of Soberton and Newtown until the 1970s.

The Junor Family

Robert Junor, a retired RN Lieutenant Commander and formerly an engineer on the Royal yacht, lived with his wife, Florence, in Flint Cottage, Chapel Road.

Although their older son, Hugh, did not have a direct Swanmore connection, Cecil, the younger one – a keen photographer – was a familiar figure at the biennial reunions of the old Swanmorians from the mid-1960s onwards.

Both sons attained considerable distinction. Hugh was pilot to Lawrence of Arabia in World War I and mentioned on various occasions in Lawrence's book *The Seven Pillars of Wisdom*. During the early- and mid-1920s Hugh became a test pilot for the Royal Aeronautical Establishment at Farnborough, helping to develop the forerunners of the aircraft that were eventually to prove so decisive in our success in World War II. Sadly Hugh was killed in a flying accident in 1926.

Robert H and Florence (right) Junor.

Cecil, for his part, trained as a marine electrical engineer, serving an apprenticeship with Swan Hunter. During World War II he worked on oil tankers and was severely wounded when on duty in the Mediterranean, subsequently spending a long time in hospital in Alexandria. Cecil was awarded the MBE for his bravery during this incident. He had earlier married Eileen Spurr, the daughter of the licensee of the Mafeking Hero public house in

Bishop's Waltham. The couple, who lived in Waltham Chase during the war, had twin daughters, Mary and Celia, and a younger one named Pat. When he retired at the age of 65 in the 1960s he became a part-time lecturer at the Southampton College of Technology, where he carried on working until the age of 80.

Robert, his father, died aged 75 in February 1948 on the same day as his drinking companion of many years, Fred Marsh Snr (aged 66). Both were buried at St Barnabas Church on St Valentine's Day.

Hugh Junor's wedding.

94

Cecil Junor.

A Date to Remember
by Ron Crook

Ron Crook and his best pal Eric were out in the streets of Hampshire enjoying the VE Day celebrations, but it turned out to be a date to remember in more ways than one. Here is his account of what happened:

Marie Crook.

"Later in the evening of course we all adjourned to the bar.... and we all went into the dance hall and there was this delightful young lady there. I was a bit shy but I approached her and said would you have a drink. [6]

"Soon after that, two of her friends arrived in a car—although it was difficult to get petrol—and said 'would you like to come with us?' We toured down through a lot of the villages in Hampshire and particularly Wickham—into Wickham Square.

"They had a great do there with a band and everyone was dancing, and the beer was flowing out of all the pubs—most of it free fortunately—and I danced with her, and my memory is that we danced to one of the musical tunes You are the Honeysuckle and I am the Bee. And that's a memory that stays in my mind.

"I asked if I could meet her again later on—and she agreed to do that—and from then on we were going out together for at least four years and we were married in 1949. For 56 years we had a superbly happy life—and she was a great lady. And coincidently our first house, which was a rented house, was in Wickham Square.

"I remember asking her some years later, 'What did you really see in me?'—because I was a bit raw back then. And she said, 'Well you were not a bad looking sort of chap and there's probably some material I could mould into shape.' And she was dead right of course.

"I still say that she still influences me—not sadly but otherwise—and as I said, she was a great lady—and that's my story of VE Day."

<hr>

[6] Ron's wife to be was Marie Trigg.

Ron and Marie Crook.

Wedding of Alma Edney to George Parsons at Swanmore Methodist Church, 1950.

Recreation Ground - races.

Recreation Ground - races.

Swanmore Primary School, 1946.
Back: Jean Beckinsale, Vivian Mockler, Iris Messam, Joan Harvey, June Gibson, Janet Lock, Marguerite Gough
Next: Stanley Hibberd, Gerald Doyle, ?, Dennis Elliot, David Crouch, Clive Emery, Reginald Boswell,
Gavin Maidment, Dave Newton, Douglas Read
Sitting: ?, Donald Godwin, Margaret Emery, ?, Richard Watson, Kenneth Gillard,
Front: Edwin Hughes, Harold (Rumbold) Rumble, Roy Lipscombe, Bob Harvey?, Anthony Mills, ?, Douglas Adams.

Swanmore Youth Club with their leader, Miss Margaret Belbin (2nd from left standing), on a trip to London. They stayed at a hostel in Devonshire Street belonging to the National Association of Girls Clubs and Mixed Clubs, to which the club was affiliated. June Clarkson (née Gillard), Front 2nd Left - Vera Tribbeck (Extreme Rt-Standing)

Workers at the Cortursel factory on New Road.
Back: Audrey Apps, Pamela Smith, Margaret Langford, Arch Denton, Joan Privett, Evelyn Belstone, Nancy Dredge,
Maureen Sessions Middle: Dorothy Eyles, Mabel Woods
Seated: Doris Veck, Margaret Hazzard, Violet Wilkinson, Mrs Godwin Front:Alan Woods

Worker at the Cortursel factory on New Road.

Back: Eve Smith, Joyce Emmott, Ann Smith, Don Godwin, Reggie Moore, Sonny Barney

Middle: Dorothy Eyles, Edna Petty, Sheila Bound

Front: Sheila Smith, Sylvia West, Violet Wilkinson, Ivy Searle, Margaret Avery, Hilda Cook, Kathleen Toone, Eva ?, Joan Hazzard, Pam Smith,

Melda Beckett, Mabel Woods.

*Southern Evening Echo
report on the Timothy Whites
& Taylors blaze, May 1948.*

TUESDAY   MAY   4,   1948

BIG BLAZE AT SWANMORE

Chemists' Hardware Store Gutted

"Echo" Staff Reporter

SEVEN full huts forming part of Timothy Whites and Taylors hardware warehouse at Swanmore were burned to the ground last night, causing damage running into five figures.

Lawnmowers, combustion stoves, medicinal goods, tap washers, oil stoves, tins of turpentine, and a miscellany of household goods fell victims to the flames, which could be seen miles away. Firemen worked throughout the night on the outbreak.

"COVER" FOR FIREMEN

The firemen found it impossible, when they arrived, to get near the building because of the terrific heat, and used a trailer-wagon that stood nearby as fire-cover while they played jets on the scorched house 50ft. away from the actual blaze, and then smashed the fully-loaded vehicles into safety.

Cardboard boxes began smouldering behind the melting windows of the house which forms the main part of the store building. The boxes were dumped just in time to prevent the fire spreading to highly-inflammable medicinal preparations kept in the house. The cause of the fire is at present unknown.

HOUSE SAVED

Ten part-time retained personnel from Bishop's Waltham, under Station Officer C. E. Pink, were first on the scene, and it was their prompt action which saved the house.

Droxford, Wickham, Titchfield, Warsash, Botley, Eastleigh and Winchester appliances were in attendance. Lt-Col. A. de P. Kingsmill, chairman of the Hampshire Fire Committee, was visiting fire stations in the vicinity at the time, and he visited the spot, with Hampshire's Chief Officer A. W. Paramor, Deputy Chief Officer A. E. Bowles and Divisional Officer H. F. Griffiths.

100

Walter Downer Landlord of The New Inn throughout WWII with his grandchildren Bill and Philippa Watson. Circa 1952.

Cecil ('Pop') and Edith Willing, 1955.

Appendix A: Swanmore Electoral Register:
Extract of Service Voters 1939
Hampshire Record Office H/CL/4/328

	Arthur William Archer	Mayfield, New Road
	Albert Humphrey Bott	New Road
	Robert Bruce Bound	Southcote, Chapel Road
	Edward George Brown	West Dene, New Road
	Douglas Edward Clarebolt	St Heliers, Forest Road
	Harry George Coffin	1 Spion Kop
	John Emmott	South Cottage, Hill Cross
*	Ernest William Farr	Swanmore Park Cottages
*	Cecil Hugh George	South View
*	Harry Gomer	Spring Lane
	Reginald Arthur Gomer	Watsons Bungalows
	Charles Stanley Griffin	Swanmore Park, Upper Swanmore
	Ernest Henry Hall	2 Sunnyside, Lower Chase Road
	Reginald Hibberd	Neva Cottage, New Road
	Percy Jestico Hickmott	6 Council Cottages
	Reginald Percy George Knight	Hill Cross
	Herbert James Leamon	The Firs, Upper Swanmore
*	Christopher Gordon Light	Belmont House
	Arthur George Mack	Donigers
	Richard Paston Mack	Donigers
	William Richard Marshall	The Hollies
	Thomas Nevil Masterman	Aherlow Cottage
	Robert Henry Mockler	Growthorne, Chapel Road
	Frederick Edward Newman	Laurel Cottage, Chapel Road
	Reginald John Newnham	Holmwood, Chapel Road
	Henry Sherborne Percival	The Lakes
	Harry Robert Randall	Ludwell's Corner, Waltham Chase
	Richard Cyril Roberts	Coronel, Chapel Road
	John James Tayler	The Hunters Inn
	Claude Vivien Webster	Newton Cottage
	Leslie Harold Willoughby	Primrose Cottage, Dodds Lane

Reg Newnham at the Hunter's Inn. He was based at No 3 Depot PFA Hillsea in 1915.

Reg Newnham, 2nd Lt in World War II.

* Denotes killed in World War II. Full details in the Swanmore War Memorial Remembrance Book.

On Behalf of His Majesty's Government I wish to thank you for the service you have rendered to the nation during the war. The task of British agriculture, an arduous, indeed a vital one, was to keep the nation fed. With your help it has been done.

W.A.E.C's by their care and consideration, secured the willing co-operation of the farming community, and have, by their energy and example, raised the production of our farms to a new high level.

I am confident you will always be proud of having played so important a part in the contribution which British agriculture has made to our Victory.

Minister of Agriculture and Fisheries,
8th May 1945.

To E. Watson Esq.,
Supplementary District Committee member of the Hampshire War Agricultural Executive Committee.

Appendix C: Royal letter of thanks to those who sheltered evacuees

E R

I WISH TO MARK, BY THIS PERSONAL MESSAGE, my appreciation of the service you have rendered to your Country in 1939.

In the early days of the War you opened your door to strangers who were in need of shelter, & offered to share your home with them.

I know that to this unselfish task you have sacrificed much of your own comfort, & that it could not have been achieved without the loyal co-operation of all in your household.

By your sympathy you have earned the gratitude of those to whom you have shown hospitality, & by your readiness to serve you have helped the State in a work of great value.

Elizabeth R

Editors Footnote

Kath Reed (née Horner) now in her 90's but then a young wife and mother was among the villagers who received this message from Queen Elizabeth (wife of King George the VITH.)

Kath's two evacuees came from Gosport.

Appendix D: Swanmore Invasion Committee War Book

An invasion committee was formed under the chairmanship of Mrs Maurice (Ethel) Portal of Holywell. They compiled a directory of useful information, called the Invasion Committee War Book. Each page is duplicated (by using carbon paper), and for many of the pages even the top sheet is a carbon copy of another document. The book used has an index at the front, which has been filled in, and the pages are pre-numbered. For rapid indexing, tabs have been stuck on each section.

The major part of the book is reproduced in the follow pages together with a local directory which was incorporated therein note page 29 was completely blank.

To set the scene, here is part of a Government leaflet on what to do if an invasion happened.

Issued by the Ministry of Information in co-operation with the War Office *and the Ministry of Home Security.*

If the

INVADER

comes

WHAT TO DO — AND HOW TO DO IT

THE Germans threaten to invade Great Britain. If they do so they will be driven out by our Navy, our Army and our Air Force. Yet the ordinary men and women of the civilian population will also have their part to play. Hitler's invasions of Poland, Holland and Belgium were greatly helped by the fact that the civilian population was taken by surprise. They did not know what to do when the moment came. *You must not be taken by surprise.* This leaflet tells you what general line you should take. More detailed instructions will be given you when the danger comes nearer. Meanwhile, read these instructions carefully and be prepared to carry them out.

I

When Holland and Belgium were invaded, the civilian population fled from their homes. They crowded on the roads, in cars, in carts, on bicycles and on foot, and so helped the enemy by preventing their own armies from advancing against the invaders. You must not allow that to happen here. Your first rule, therefore, is :—

(1) IF THE GERMANS COME, BY PARACHUTE, AEROPLANE OR SHIP, YOU MUST REMAIN WHERE YOU ARE. THE ORDER IS "STAY PUT ".

If the Commander in Chief decides that the place where you live must be evacuated, he will tell you when and how to leave. Until you

receive such orders you must remain where you are. If you run away, you will be exposed to far greater danger because you will be machine-gunned from the air as were civilians in Holland and Belgium, and you will also block the roads by which our own armies will advance to turn the Germans out.

II

There is another method which the Germans adopt in their invasion. They make use of the civilian population in order to create confusion and panic. They spread false rumours and issue false instructions. In order to prevent this, you should obey the second rule, which is as follows :—

(2) DO NOT BELIEVE RUMOURS AND DO NOT SPREAD THEM. WHEN YOU RECEIVE AN ORDER, MAKE QUITE SURE THAT IT IS A TRUE ORDER AND NOT A FAKED ORDER. MOST OF YOU KNOW YOUR POLICEMEN AND YOUR A.R.P. WARDENS BY SIGHT, YOU CAN TRUST THEM. IF YOU KEEP YOUR HEADS, YOU CAN ALSO TELL WHETHER A MILITARY OFFICER IS REALLY BRITISH OR ONLY PRETENDING TO BE SO. IF IN DOUBT ASK THE POLICE-MAN OR THE A.R.P. WARDEN. USE YOUR COMMON SENSE.

Government information leaflet: "If the Invader comes" (first page).

SWANMORE INVASION COMMITTEE

CHAIRMAN. = M~rs~ MAURICE PORTAL. HOLYWELL
    TEL: DROXFORD 21.

HOME GUARD = ~~LT. F. RUDD~~ LT. M. MACFARLANE.
    TEL. BISHOPS WALTHAM. ~~56~~ 173.

SENIOR WARDEN = M~r~ E.W. JACOBS. CHAPEL ROAD.
    NO TELEPHONE.

POLICE = P.C. NICHOLSON. CHURCH ROAD.
    TEL. BISHOPS WALTHAM. 225

FOOD (r.Hon.Sec.) = M~rs~ GADSBY. ROSE COTTAGE. Upper Swanmore
    TEL. BISHOPS WALTHAM 158

A.R.P. WARDEN = MAJOR MAURICE PORTAL. D.S.O. HOLYWELL
    TEL. DROXFORD. 21.

    M~r~ E. WATSON. HILL GROVE FARM.
    TEL. DROXFORD. 35.

DEPUTY CHAIRMÆN = { Rev. E.S. Wakefield. The Vicarage SWANMORE
    { M~r~ E.W. ELDRED. SWANMORE HOUSE. B.W. 230.

FIRE GUARDS = M~r~ H.C. WAINWRIGHT. "WEE HAME"
    HILL POUND.

CASUALTY SERVICE = M~rs~ A.H. LAW. Jervis Lodge.
    TEL: BISHOPS W: 162.

PARISH H.Q. (~~L.D.E.~~) INVASION CTTEE
(Boy's Club) PARISH ROOM

HOME GUARD H.Q   Church R^d ~~Tel~~.
                                    Draper's Farm Tel. 152
      O.P.   Tel. B.W. 153.

POLICE H.Q SWANMORE.   CHURCH RD.
                    TEL. BISHOPS WALTHAM 225

A.R.P. H.Q   (Boy's CLUB) PARISH ROOM

FIRE GUARD. H.Q
                        (Boy's CLUB) PARISH ROOM

Tab labels (right margin):
INVASION CTTEE A.R.P H.Q parish H.Q
1st AID POINT HOSPITALS MEMBERS
EMERGENCY
A.R.P. WARDENS.
FIRE GUARDS.
SECTOR ORGANISERS (LABOUR)
MANPOWER & TOOLS TRANSPORT
REST CENTRES
WATER. SUPPLY.
FOOD.
BURIALS

FIRST AID POINT.

In Charge:- <u>M^{RS} A.H. LAW.</u> Jervis Lodge
TEL. BISHOPS WALTHAM 162.

<u>H.Q. British Legion Hall.</u> New Road.

STAFF.

M^{RS} Draper.	Upper Swanmore.	TEL.	B-W.152
M^{RS} Doyle.	Burlington Villas.		
M^{RS} Carpenter.	5 Moorland Rd.		
M^{RS} Green	Hill Top.	"	B-W.153
M^{RS} Gough	6 Moorland Rd.		
M^{RS} Gray	Vicarage Lane.		
Miss Nickels.	" "	"	B-W. 149
M^{RS} Merritt	Church R^d	"	B-W 3
Miss L. Tier	Chapel R^d		
M^{RS} Warren.	Mayhill	"	Drox. 130
Miss B. Watson	Hill Pound	"	B-W 107
Miss J. Watson	" "	"	" "
M^{RS} Whitaker	Church R^d		
M^{RS} Taylor White.	Hampton Hill	"	B-W. 38
MR E.W. Jacobs	Chapel R^d		
MR Wainwright.	Wee Hame. Hill Pound.		
MR H. Merritt	12 Council Hses.		
MR Hughes.	Hampton Hill Cottage		
MR Ainsley	Hill Pound		
MR Evans.	Primrose Cottage		
MR Tilbury	Sunny View. B-W. R^d		

Emergency Dressing Station

The Schools & Church.

Emergency Hospitals

Holywell.	Tel. Drox:	21.
Hill Place	" "	68
Swanmore House	" B-W.	230
" Vicarage	" B-W	
Hunters Inn Hall		

A. R. P. SERVICE

<u>CHIEF WARDEN</u>:- Mr E.W. Jacobs. Chapel Rd.

Headquarters   PARISH ROOM.

<u>WARDENS</u>.

   <u>Mr Pratt</u>. (Bricklayers Arms)

      <u>Sector</u> Bricklayers Inn to Moorlands Rd. including part of Lower Chase Rd.

   <u>Mr Ellis</u> (Hampton Hill)

      <u>Sector</u> Upper Swanmore to Swanmore House

   <u>Mr A.V. Page</u>. (Church Rd)

      <u>Sector</u>. NEW Rd. and part of FOREST Rd

   <u>Mrs Robinson</u>.

      <u>Sector</u>. Hunters Inn to Gravel Hill including part FOREST Rd.

   <u>Mr H. MERRITT</u>.

      <u>Sector</u>. HILL Pound, Spring Lane and DODD Lane.

   <u>Mr W. Adams</u>.

      <u>Sector</u> Vicarage Lane and part of Church Rd.

   MAJOR M. PORTAL. HOLYWELL

      <u>Sector</u>. Mislingford to Jones' St Clair's Farm to Tudor Cottage (COTT Sr)

A.R.P. WARDENS. | FIRE GUARDS. | SECTOR ORGANISERS (LABOUR) | MANPOWER & TOOLS TRANSPORT | REST CENTRES | Water Supply | FOOD | BURIALS

FIRE GUARDS.

Senior Fire Guard.

Mr Wainwright. Wee Hame. Hill Pound.

Sector Wardens

A. Merritt. Centre of village.

Miss Watson. New Road.

Mrs Gough. Moorlands Road.

Mr Dyer Lower Chase Road.

Mr Benham. Forest Road.

Rev. A. Brown Vicarage Lane.

H. C. Wainwright Hill Pound.

FIRE GUARDS. | SECTOR ORGANISERS (LABOUR) | MANPOWER & TOOLS TRANSPORT | REST CENTRES SUPPLY. | Water. Food. | BURIALS

SECTOR ORGANISATION
(LABOUR)

Sector Organisers

Sector I. { F. Smith (Cott Sᵗ Farm and   Tel. DROX.III
{ E. Watson (Hill Grove)   Tel. DROX 35

Cott Sᵗ (Sinclairs Frm.) via Hunter's Inn to
Hill Pound X Rᵈˢ (Tribbeck's)

Sector 2. F. Horn. (Upper Hill Frm)
Droxford Rᵈ to Hunters X Rᵈˢ (Dodd Lane)

Sector 3. { F. Clarke (LITTLE Nest Frm)
{ H. Warren (Mayhill)   Tel.
Hunter's X Rᵈˢ (DODD Lane) - Vicarage Lane -
Upper Swanmore (junction Hampton Hill) & MAYhill

Sector 4. A. J. Vincent. (Parish Room)
Swanmore Hill, Church Rᵈ, Chapel Kᵃ
to Hill Pound.

Sector 5 G. SAVAGE. (Holywell)
Mislingford (junc: DROX :- WICKHAM Rᵈ) to
HILL Pound.

Sector 6. { MORGAN (Wassail Hut)
{ MOULD (HAWK'S Nest)
Mislingford X Rds to Gravel Hill.

P.T.O.

<u>Sector Organisation. (Labour) cont'd</u>

<u>Sector 7.</u> MR A.G. SMITH
GRAVEL HILL TO HILL POUND (TRIBBECK's)

<u>Sector 8</u> { MR PARRINGTON.
MR W.O. KNIGHT
FOREST Rd (Gravel Hill X Rds) TO THE CHASE

<u>Sector 9</u> { MR CHATTERS (THE Lakes)
NEW Rd. Brickworks (MR HEATH)
NEW RD (from Martin's Corner To Junc! FOREST Rd

<u>Sector 10.</u> { MR L. DRAPER (HOME Farm) TEL. B.W. 152
MR E.W. ELDRED (SWANMORE Hse Tel " 230
Shepherds Down to bottom of
HAMPTON HILL

<u>Sector 11</u> { MR F. MARSH. Avoca.
MR DADSWELL. LOWER Chase
MR W. Singleton. " "
LOWER CHASE Rd. to Junc! the Chase
including LUDWELLS.

<u>Sector 12</u> MR DAYSH. MOORLANDS Rd.
Donigers Dell to Hoe Rd including
MOORLANDS RD.
P.T.O.

Sector Organisation (LABOUR)

I <u>Sector Organisers</u> are <u>responsible</u> for <u>all roads</u> in their <u>Sector</u>. They recruit <u>own Labour</u>, and are ready to turn out with labour and <u>tools</u> upon receipt of <u>message</u> (per messenger service) from Parish H.Q, <u>or</u> to act on <u>their own</u> responsibility -

II Each Sector "<u>locks</u>" with another in the Parish, or with the adjoining Parish. ALL Sector Organisers to be prepared to transfer their labour to <u>another Sector</u> if <u>need arises</u>.

SECTOR MANPOWER &
TRANSPORT & TOOLS

F.SMITH   SECTOR I   E WATSON

DAY	TRANSPORT	NIGHT	TOOLS	
(MEN) 13	3 horses	6	prongs	18
	6 carts		spades	18
			shovels	10
			picks	4
			grub axes	4
			barrows	6
			ladders	4
			crowbars	2

F. HORN   Sector 2

DAY	TRANSPORT	NIGHT	TOOLS	
3	1 horse	3	prongs	2
	1 cart		spades	2
			shovels	2
			picks	1
			grubaxes	
			barrows	1
			ladders	2

F. Clarke   Sector 3   H. Warren

DAY	TRANSPORT	NIGHT	TOOLS	
7	2 horses	3	prongs	4
	1 cart		spades	13
			shovels	10
			picks	
			barrows	7
			adze	1
			ladders	8
			crowbars	4
			rammers	1

A.J.Vincent   Sector 4

DAY	TRANSPORT	NIGHT	TOOLS	
	2 horses	4	prongs	4
	1 FLOAT		spades	4
			picks	2
			shovels	4
			grubaxes	
			crowbars	2
			barrows	4
			ladders	4

SECTOR MANPOWER & (Cont<u>d</u>)
TRANSPORT. & TOOLS

C.SAVAGE   Sector 5

	DAY	TRANSPORT	NIGHT. TOOLS
(MEN.)	6	2 horses 3 carts	5. prongs..6 spades..6 shovels..2 picks...2 barrows..2 ladders..3 crowbars..1

Morgan   Sector 6

DAY	TRANSPORT	NIGHT. TOOLS
4	2 horses 2 carts	4. prongs...9 spades...6 shovels...9 picks...0 barrows...2 ladders...5 crowbars...3

A.G.SMITH   Sector 7

DAY	TRANSPORT	NIGHT TOOLS
4		4. prongs... spades...4 shovels... picks... barrows...6 ladders...6 crowbars..1 rammers..2 graft...1

W.O.KNIGHT.   Sector 8

DAY	TRANSPORT	NIGHT TOOLS
6	1 horse 1 cart	6. prongs..4 spades.... shovels...3 picks....2 barrows...2 ladders...2 rammers..2

Sector Manpower & Transport & Tools

CHATTERS. Sector 9

DAY	TRANSPORT	NIGHT	TOOLS
(Men) 10-19	2 horses	9	prongs . . 12
	1 carts		spades . . 6
			shovels . 10
			picks . . . 6
			barrows . 3
			ladders . 3
			crowbars . 3
			rammers . 2

L. DRAPER. Sector 10   E. ELDRED.

DAY	TRANSPORT	NIGHT	TOOLS
16	4 horses	7	prongs . 12
	5 carts		spades . 12
			shovels . 12
			picks . 24
			barrows . 2
			ladders . 12
			crowbars . 6
			rammers . 2

DADSWELL   Sector 11   W. SINGLETON.

DAY	TRANSPORT	NIGHT	TOOLS
5	3 horses	5	prongs . . 11
	3 carts		spades . . .
	1 trolley		shovels . . 8
			picks . . 6
			barrows . . 3
			ladders . 2
			crowbars . 2
			rammers . 2

J. DAYSH   Sector 12

DAY	TRANSPORT	NIGHT	TOOLS
		6	prongs . 4
			spades . 6
			shovels . 10
			picks . 2
			barrows . 4
			ladders . 3
			crowbars . 3
			rammers . 1

REST CENTRES (PARISH OFFICER: Mrs Portal
(Establishments Officer:- Mr Whitaker
(Information Officer:- Mrs Whitaker

I PARISH ROOM.
To be used as a Feeding Centre.
Accommodation for   persons.

KITCHEN EQUIPMENT.
1 gas cooker.
2 boiling stoves for use outdoors; to burn coal or wood.

REST CENTRES (contd)

BRITISH LEGION HALL

SLEEPING ACCOMODATION FOR 120 PERSONS.

EQUIPMENT.
120   mattresses
620   blankets   } Stored at LINTERS* CHAPEL Rd
24   beds.   } (Key)

4   hurricane lamps

REST CENTRES (contd)

BRICKLAYERS HALL

REST CENTRES   (Cont'd)

STAFF

PARISH OFFICER :- MRS M. PORTAL. HOLYWELL
  DEPUTY :-   MRS Whitbourn. Coronel.

MRS Wellstead	Council Houses
MRS Stubbington	Hillgrove Cottages
MRS Vincent	Parish Room.
MRS Butcher	1 Council Houses
Miss L.F. Taylor	Rose Cottage.
MRS Clive	Mayes Cottage
MRS Beckett	Westwood
MRS Brown	Vicarage
MRS Green	Hill Top.
MRS Westbrook.	Hampton Hill
MRS Phelps	Myrtle Cottage
MRS W. Clarke	Council House
MRS Strick	Tudor Cottage
MRS H. Watson	Jervis Crt. Farm.
MRS Boswell	" " Cottages
MRS Didymus	Council Houses
MRS Wort	Rectory Cottage
MRS Dadswell.	Fields Frm. Lower Chase
MRS Underwood	
MRS Hatch	Hiawatha.
MRS Moore	Tin Cottage

WATER SUPPLY.

In the event of a breakdown in the piped water supply from the Gosport Water Works, an EMERGENCY SUPPLY can be obtained from Wells.

All water from Wells should be <u>boiled</u> for 5 (FIVE) MINUTES.

LIST OF USABLE WELLS

MR MARSH. THE DELL.
MR Crouch Rose Cottage. Swanmore Hill
M^{RS} KNIGHT   "   "
MR Pratt.   Bricklayer's Arms   "   "

MR DADSWELL   LOWER CHASE RD
MR SINGLETON   "   "   "
MR M^C NEILL   BROAD LANE, NEW RD.
MR ROBERTS. CORONEL, Chapel RD.
M^{RS} Edney (SEN) Spring Lane.
                    ~~Spring well in Spring Lane~~
M^{RS} WILLIAMS. Burlington Villas.
MR HORNER   Vicarage Lane
M^{RS} White   Bucket Farm.

Water Food Supply.

BURIALS

FOOD SUPPLIES

Voluntary Food Organiser : MRS H. GADSBY.

Deputy. Mrs E.W. Eldred   Rose Cottage. Upper Swanmore
    Swanmore House, Tel.B.W. 230.   Tel. B-W. 158

EMERGENCY FOOD COMMITTEE
V.F.O. MRS Gadsby.
- MR H. MERRITT.   (Grocers)
- MR E. KERTON   (BUTCHERS)
- MR TRIBBECK   (Bakers)

COASTAL BELT   <u>RATIONS</u> (distribution points :—
- I Old MISSION HALL. NEW ROAD
- II HOLYWELL.
- III SWANMORE COTTAGE.
  - <u>N.B.</u> ONLY TO BE ISSUED WHEN SUPPLIES IN SHOPS ARE EXHAUSTED.

<u>RETAILERS.</u>
<u>GROCERS</u> :- MR H. MERRITT. MID-HANTS STORES
         MR H. MARTIN. MARTIN'S STORES
         MR BABBIDGE NEW RD
         MR TRIBBECK HILL POUND
         MRS FRY   CHURCH RD

<u>BUTCHERS</u> :- MR E. KERTON. NEW Rd.
         MR TIBBLE   CHAPEL Rd.

FOOD

BURIALS

FOOD SUPPLIES (CONT?)

<u>RETAILERS</u> (cont^d)

   <u>BAKERS</u> :- MR TRIBBECK.   HILL POUND

<u>EMERGENCY BAKERY</u> :- MID-HANTS STORES.
   (EMERGENCY FUEL SUPPLY IN SITU)

<u>MILK PRODUCERS</u>

<u>W. MESSAM</u>.	Mislingford.	9	COWS.	av: 14-16	g/l.p.d
<u>W. PARRINGTON</u>.	Forest R^d	15	"	" 30	gl:p.d.
<u>CHATTERS</u>	THE LAKES	8	"	" 16	galls.p.d.
<u>F. MARSH</u>.	THE Dell	13	"	25	" . .
<u>E. WATSON</u>	Hill Grove.	48	"	100	" . .
~~H. TIBBLE~~.	~~Chapel R^d~~	~~4~~	"	~~6~~	" . .
<u>F. CLARKE</u>	Little Nest	13		18	" . .
<u>F. SMITH</u>		8		8-10	" . .

                        18   217   ?TO

FOOD SUPPLY   Cont^d

MILK PRODUCERS

	COWS	Av: galls p.d.
Major M. PORTAL. HOLYwell.	4	8
M^R FRY. Spring Lane	6	10
MR DADSWELL. Fields Farm.	10	15
MR F. HORN. Upper Hill Farm.	15	30
MR W. Singleton LOWER Chase R^d	4	6
MR L. DRAPER. Home Farm.	26	50
MR H. WATSON. Jervis Gt. Frm.		
MR MORGAN. Wassail Hall	10	15-18
MR WATSON ~~Mould~~ Hawks Nest.		
TOTALS	183	435

FOOD SUPPLY. (cont'd)

(a) All retailers now carry 14 days reserve stocks in addition to their current stocks.

(b) 8 days' emergency rations are held in the Coastal Belt Reserves.

PLANS for DISTRIBUTION of C.B.R.

Method of distribution must depend on the extent of the emergency then ruling. The scattered nature of the village renders any plan difficult to operate in disturbed conditions. Postcards addresses to every householder telling him the Point at which rations are to be collected, are in readiness, & will be posted if postal service is working.

OTHER MEANS OF INFORMING THE PUBLIC.

a) By Cyclist Messenger Corps
b) PUBLIC NOTICES in conjunction with POLICE
c) Through WARDENS SERVICE or FIRE GUARDS.

DISTRIBUTION FROM POINTS

IF conditions allow distribution will be made from the C.B.R. Points already mentioned. Skeleton staffs for the Points are ready & it is hoped to augment these from among the people whose normal work will cease under Invasion conditions.

SEE OVER

FOOD SUPPLY (cont^{td})

DISTRIBUTION OF C.B.R. (Con^{td})

OTHER MEANS OF DISTRIBUTION.

N.B. IF traffic in certain areas is CLOSED by MILITARY AUTHORITIES, it is their responsibility to make alternative arrangements to enable V.F.O to carry out distribution.

IN an EXTREME EMERGENCY distribution will be made by any means available, as equitably as possible to the population, so as to deny food stocks to the enemy as far as possible. All those to whom food is issued will be warned to hide their supplies.

To AFFECT DISTRIBUTION use will be made of any form of transport available.

THE COMMITTEE of SHOPKEEPERS already formed will assist the V.F.O. & have been informed as to the general scheme which will operate if the V.F.O. has to assume control in this area.

EMERGENCY BURIALS

In the event of numerous fatal casualties, trenches will be dug by the Labour Group under Mr Vincent (Sector 4); coffins will be dispensed with.

It is planned to dig these trenches in the <u>Allotment Field</u> on the right of <u>Vicarage Lane</u>.

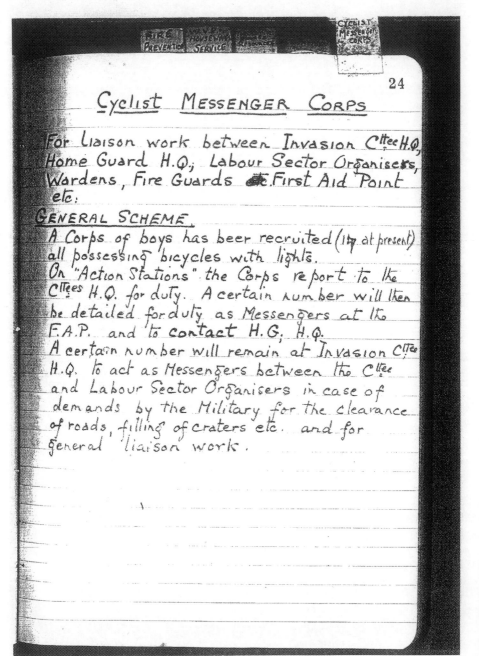

Cyclist Messenger Corps

For Liaison work between Invasion Cttee H.Q,
Home Guard H.Q.; Labour Sector Organisers,
Wardens, Fire Guards & First Aid Point
etc.

GENERAL SCHEME.

A Corps of boys has been recruited (14 at present)
all possessing bicycles with lights.

On "Action Stations" the Corps report to the
Cttees H.Q. for duty. A certain number will then
be detailed for duty as Messengers at the
F.A.P. and to contact H.G. H.Q.

A certain number will remain at Invasion Cttee
H.Q. to act as Messengers between the Cttee
and Labour Sector Organisers in case of
demands by the Military for the clearance
of roads, filling of craters etc. and for
general liaison work.

CYCLIST MESSENGER CORPS.

NAMES.

P. Marsh.	Avoca. Bishops Waltham Rd.
R. Crouch.	Rose Cottage. Swanmore Hill.
J. Jacobs.	Ivy Cott. Lower Chase Rd.
A. Wort.	Hill Grove Cottages.
P. Kirby.	Ferndale, Brickyard.
R. Parker.	The Laurels, New Rd.
J. Wellstead.	Council Houses, Chapel Rd.
~~R. Jeffreys,~~	~~Hill Pound.~~
R. J. Snook,	Broadlands, Chapel Rd.
G. A. Kerley.	Holmwood, Chapel Rd.
P. Parsons.	Hill Pound.
C. Parsons	Vicarage Lane.
R. Laws.	Hill Grove Cottages.
R. French.	Holywell.
G. Farr.	Vicarage Lane
E. Madden.	
G. Adams.	Council Houses.

<u>ACTION</u> to be taken by <u>INVASION</u> C<u>ttee</u> on
          receipt of "<u>STAND TO</u>" warning:-
<u>COMMITTEE</u> <u>MEETS</u> and reviews plans,
bringing them up-to-date if necessary.
Displays poster, enjoining <u>STAND FIRM</u> policy.
<u>ACTION</u> on receipt of "<u>ACTION STATIONS</u>":-
    <u>INVASION</u> H.Q. manned during the 24
hours by <u>CHAIRMAN</u> and <u>DEPUTIES</u>.
Shifts will be of 8 hours with an overlap
of ½ hours to ensure continuity.
The Chairman or Deputy on duty will at
once contact H.G. Headquarters and
maintain liaison by means of Messenger Corps,
as long as possible.

POPULATION, HOUSES, & RESOURSES.

The population of SWANMORE taken in
Oct. 1941, including people sleeping in the
village at night r at week-ends (temporarily) was: 1,788

Number of households approx: = 397

RESOURSES

There are Two wholesale warehouses
in the village. i.e.

Messrs TIMOTHY WHITES & TAYLORS
SWANMORE HOUSE. (Food, Medical stores etc)

Messrs. R r J. SNOOK (wholesale grocers)
Church Rd

COAL & COKE.

Messrs. TIMOTHY Whites have a fairly
large supply.

WOOD. Major Portal Holywell has circular saw
r supplies of wood cut r uncut.
Mr A.J. Mills, Highfield. Upper SWANMORE has
circular saw r supply of wood.

W.V.S. HOUSEWIVES SERVICE

Scheme under review

FIRE PREVENTION. cont.

FIRE GUARDS under M<u>r</u> H.C. WAINWRIGHT
   All FIRE PARTIES have STIRRUP PUMPS
and some form of WATER CONTAINERS to
keep up a supply of WATER.

Two MAN MANUAL PUMP and hose.
   This has recently been supplied.
Housed at :- MERRITT'S SHED.

Another TWO-MAN MANUAL PUMP is
stationed at MESSrs TIMOTHY WHITES
at SWANMORE HOUSE, where there is a
good independent water supply from
underground tanks and wells.

WATER SUPPLY
IF MAINS ARE BROKEN this presents
a problem. THERE IS ONE SURFACE WELL
in SPRING LANE (UNFIT for drinking).
ONE POND at Upper SWANMORE.

See OVER.

FIRE PREVENTION cont^d

BUCKET-CHAIN SQUADS seem the only method of supplying Fire Parties from wells.

WATER CARTS.

Mr L. DRAPER. HOME FARM. UPPER SWANMORE
Mr H. GADSBY. ROSE COTTAGE " "
Mr E. WATSON HILL GROVE FARM. (2)

Editors Footnote

The original copy of the Swanmore Invasion Committee War Book was presented to Swanmore Archives by Invasion Committee member Mrs Gadsby in 2003, together with the following Air Raid Wardens and the Droxford Rural District Address list.

Air Raid Wardens up to Date 7.12.42

E.W. Jacobs. Parish Warden Chapel Road Swanmore
Major. M. Postal Holywell
Mr W. Adams. 3 Council House
Mr E. Whitbourn Chapel Road
Mr J Ellis Hampton Hill
Mr J. Pratt Bricklayers arms
Mrs. M. Robinson Hill Pound
Mr. Whyatt Hill Pound
Mr Eric Reeves The Hollies Vicarage Lane } New
Mr W. Mouland upper Swanmore } Members
Mr Brown. Moelands Road

A.R.P. Headquarters.
The Square, Bishop's Waltham, Southampton. Tel.: No. 183.

Assistance Board.
" Shenstone," Portchester Road, Fareham. Tel.: No. 2261.

Billeting Officer.
Chief Billeting Officer, Council Offices. The Square, Bishop's Waltham, Southampton. Tel.: No. 180.

Parish Billeting Officers.
Bishop's Waltham.
H. M. Rogers, Esq., High Street, Bishop's Waltham, Southampton.

Boarhunt.
W. Chase, Esq., Bere Farm Lane, Boarhunt, Fareham.

Corhampton and Meonstoke and Exton.
Rev. J. Stanning, The Rectory, Meonstoke, Southampton. Tel.: No. 99.

Curbridge.
Chief Billeting Officer, Council Offices, Bishop's Waltham, Southampton. Tel.: No. 180.

Curdridge.
Col. W. M. Coldstream, Oak Avenue, Curdridge, Southampton. Tel,: Bishop's Waltham 78.

Denmead.
Chief Billeting Officer, Council Offices. Bishop's Waltham, Southampton. Tel.: No. 180.

Droxford.
A. V. Carter, Esq., High Street, Droxford, Southampton. Tel.: No. 119.

Durley.
R. M. Vaughan, Esq., Brook Cottage, Durley, Southampton.

Hambledon.
Mrs. Hall, Hill House, Hambledon, Portsmouth. Tel.: No. 24.

Shedfield.
A. R. J. Crofton, Esq. " The Shieling," Shedfield, Southampton. Tel.: Wickham 3186.

Soberton.
E. J. H. Matthews, Esq., Yew Tree Farm, Soberton, Southampton.

Southwick and Widley.
Mrs. C. J. Willoughby, The Old Vicarage, Southwick, Fareham. Tel.: Cosham 75117.

Swanmore.

Upham.
H. R. Francis. Esq., Sciviers Lane, Upham, Southampton. Tel.: Durley 15.

Warnford and Westmeon.
T. Colebourn. Esq., Bank House. Westmeon, Petersfield. Message: Westmeon 44.

Wickham.
A. E. Roberts, Esq., Frith Farm, Wickham. Fareham. Tel.: Wickham 3175.
Mrs. D. A. Warwick, Wentworth House, Wickham, Fareham. Tel.. Wickham 3750.

British Sailors' Society.
3, Orchard Place, Queen's Park, Southampton. Tel.: 3088.
Orchard Place, Southampton. Tel: 3636.

Casualty Bureau.
Council Offices, Bishop's Waltham, Southampton. Tel.: 180.

Clerk's Department.
The Clerk of the Council. The Square. Bishop's Waltham, Southampton. Tel.: 180.

Customs and Excise.
H.M. Customs and Excise Office. Osborn Road, Fareham.

Director of Navy Accounts.
The Admiralty, Whitehall, London, S.W.1.

Director of R.A.F. Accounts.
Air Ministry, Whittington Road, Worcester.

District Valuer.
Southampton.
22, Northlands Road. Tel.: 68957.
Portsmouth.
14, Penny Street. Tel.: 73677.
War Damage Claims, Telephone House. Tel.: 6006.

Divisional Petroleum Officer.
Whiteknights Park, Early, Reading. Berks.

Education Office.
The County Education Officer, The Castle, Winchester. Tel.: 1003.

Electricity.
West Hants Electricity Co., Ltd., Station Road, Bishop's Waltham, Southampton. Tel.: 100.
Mid Southern Utility Co., General Offices, Aldershot. Tel.: 800.
Portsmouth Electricity Dept., 110. High Street, Portsmouth. Tel.: 74361.

Evacuation Department.
Council Offices, Bishop's Waltham. Southampton. Tel.: 180.

Food Decontamination Officer.
Public Offices, Droxford, Southampton. Tel.: 91.

Food Office.
The Institute, Bishop's Waltham, Southampton. Tel.: 203.

Hants and Dorset Motor Services, Ltd.
12, West Street, Fareham. Tel.: 2259.

Hants Association for the Blind.
81, North Walls, Winchester. Tel.: 1503.

Hants and Isle of Wight Deaf and Dumb Association.
Miss Riddington, " Woodlands," West End, Southampton.

Health Visitors.
See list in Appendix

Hospitals.
Royal Hants County Hospital, Winchester. Tel.: 750.
Royal South Hants Hospital, Southampton. Tel.: 76211.
Shedfield Nursing Home, Shirrell Heath, Southampton. Tel.: Wickham 3172.

Information Bureau.
Council Offices, Bishop's Waltham, Southampton. Tel.: 180.

Local Fuel Overseer.
Council Offices, Bishop's Waltham, Southampton. Tel. 180.

Magistrates' Clerk's Office.
(Messrs. Gunner and Carpenter); Bank Street, Bishop's Waltham, Southampton. Tel.: 28.

Medical Officer of Health.
Public Offices, Droxford, Southampton. Tel.: 91.

Milk Officer.
Food Office, The Institute, Bishop's Waltham, Southampton. Tel.: 203.

Ministry of Health.
Insurance Dept., Pensions Records, Blackpool, Lancs. Tel.: 2541.

Ministry of Labour.
High Street, Bishop's Waltham, Southampton. Tel.: 5.

Ministry of Pensions.
Local Office Air Raid Victims, 2, Shinfield Road, Reading, Berks; or The Accountant General, Ministry of Pensions (P.I.O., I.E.), Norcross, Blackpool, Lancs.

Ministry of War Transport.
District Transport Offices.
Southampton.
22, Carlton Crescent. Tel.: 2426.
44, Northlands Road. Tel.: Bassett 68142.
Portsmouth.
Portsdown Lodge, Boundary Oak School, Purbrook, Portsmouth. Tel: Cosham 76973.

Missions to Seamen.
Queen's Terrace, Southampton. Tel.: 2106.

Mortuaries.
Northbrook, Bishop's Waltham, Southampton.
White Hart Inn, Denmead, Portsmouth.
Public Assistance Institution, Droxford, Southampton. Tel.: Droxford 45.
The Rectory, Westmeon. Petersfield. Tel.: Westmeon 26.

National Registration Office.
Council Offices, Bishop's Waltham, Southampton. Tel.: 180.

National Society for the Prevention of Cruelty to Children.
Southampton.
74, Arthur Road. Tel.: 72660.
Portsmouth.
63, Victoria Road South, Southsea.
Winchester.
Inspector Lang, 13, Worthy Lane. Message: Winchester 1861.

DROXFORD RURAL DISTRICT ADDRESS LIST

Parish Air Raid Warden.
See Appendix.

Police Stations.
See Appendix.

Portsmouth and Gosport Gas Co.
Portsmouth.
Guildhall Square, Southsea. Tel.:
Portsmouth 2185.

Bishop's Waltham.
High Street. Tel.: 9.

Portsmouth Insurance Committee.
86, Victoria Road North, Southsea.
Tel.: Portsmouth 73098.

Public Assistance.
County Public Assistance Officer, The
Castle, Winchester. Tel.: 1008.

Local Representative :—
Relieving Officer, Public Offices, Droxford, Southampton. Tel : Droxford 91.

Rating and Valuation Officer.
Council Offices, Bishop's Waltham.
Tel.: 180.

Regimental Paymaster.
If address not known write to :—
Secretary, War Office, Branch F.9,
Whitehall, London, S.W.1.

Register Office.
Council Offices, Bishop's Waltham,
Southampton. Tel.: 180.

Registrar of Births and Deaths.
F. Rudd, Esq., Public Offices, Droxford, Southampton. Tel.: Dr xford 91.

Relieving Officer.
F. Rudd, Esq., Public Offices, Droxford,
Southampton. Tel.: Droxford 91.

Rest Centres.
See Appendix.

**Royal Society for the Prevention of Cruelty
to Animals.**
Southampton.
" Monnowdene," Glenfield Crescent.
Tel.: 75204.

Portsmouth.
60, Margate Road, Southsea. Tel.:
Portsmouth 73802.

Winchester.
16, Clausentum Road. Tel.: Winchester 266.

**Soldiers', Sailors' and Airmen's Families'
Association.**
Col. W. C. P. Russell, Plas Meon,
Soberton, Southampton. Tel.: Drox-
ford 48.

Southdown Motor Services.
Hyde Park Road, Portsmouth. Tel.:
Portsmouth 74003.

Surveyor's Department.
Public Offices, Droxford, Southampton.
Tel.: Droxford 91.

War Damage Commission.
Coley Park, Reading, Berks.

Women's Voluntary Services.
See Appendix.

APPENDIX

LIST OF USEFUL ADDRESSES.

DOCTORS.

		Telephone.	
Dr. F. R. Corfe, " Elmcroft," Westmeon, Petersfield		Westmeon	33
Dr. C. P. Hemming, Bank Street, Bishop's Waltham, Southampton		Bishop's Waltham	29
Surgeon Rear-Admiral J. F. Keir, " Acorns," Winchester Road, Bishop's Waltham, South- ampton		Bishop's Waltham	147
Dr. T. G. McHattie, " Woodsmoke," Curdridge, Southampton		Botley	57
Dr. W. Drew Mitchell, Lime House, Bishop's Waltham, Southampton		Bishop's Waltham	27
Dr. J. Kinnear, Wickham House, Wickham, Fareham.		Wickham	3121
Dr. E. G. Pern, Droxford		Droxford	12
Dr. E. J. Horn, " Newlands," Denmead		Waterlooville	3264
Dr. C. H. Rock, Hill House, Hambledon, Portsmouth		Hambledon	4
Dr. Hope Murray, "Oakdene," Hambledon, Portsmouth		Hambledon	

FIRST AID POINTS.

Group 1.

BISHOP'S WALTHAM	Miss Phillips, The Rectory, Bishop's Waltham	Bishop's Waltham	123
CURDRIDGE	Dr. T. McHattie, " Woodsmoke," Curdridge	Botley	57
UPHAM	Mrs. Norton, Manor House	Durley	29
DURLEY	Mrs. Deadman, Orchard Villa, Durley	Durley	11
	(Point at Manor Road)		
SWANMORE	Mrs. Law, Jervis Lodge, Swanmore		
	(Point at Legion.)		

Group 2.

DENMEAD	Mrs. Tilbury, " Greengates," Denmead	Waterlooville	3150
HAMBLEDON	Mrs. Hall, Red House, Hambledon	Hambledon	99
SOUTHWICK	Mrs. Willoughby, The Old Vicarage, Southwick	Cosham	76586
	(Point at The Hut, Golden Lion.)		
SOBERTON	Miss F. Smith, Soberton House, Soberton	Droxford	110
,,	Mrs. Fiennes, Soberton Mill, Swanmore	Droxford	77
	(Point at Meon Place.)		

Group 3.

WICKHAM	Mrs. King, Victory Hall, Wickham	Wickham	2127
SHEDFIELD	Nurse Hearne, Cottage Hospital, Shedfield	Wickham	3172
,,	Mrs. Martin; The Vicarage, Shedfield	Wickham	2162
BOARHUNT	Mrs. Mackenzie, " Veronica," Southwick Rd, North Boarhunt	Wickham	2167
			(next door)

Group 4.

DROXFORD	Miss Happer, The Grove, Droxford	Droxford	6
WESTMEON	Mrs. Corfe, " Elmcroft," Westmeon	Westmeon	33
MEONSTOKE	Mrs. Trasenster, " Ryecroft," Meonstoke	Droxford	98
WARNFORD	Mrs. Lock, Chestnut Cottage, Warnford	Westmeon	60
	(Point at the Social Club, Old Girls' School, Warnford)		

NOTE.—All Points under-lined are also the **First Aid Depots.**

COUNTY NURSES.

Nurse Hunt, Kydale Lodge, London Road, Purbrook, Portsmouth. { Attends 1st and 3rd Fridays, 2.30, Welfare Centre, Bishop's Waltham, Congregational Chapel. Droxford, Meonstoke, Warnford, Westmeon, Swanmore, Hambledon, Denmead, Soberton are also visited.

Miss C. O. Dare, Wildgrounds, Botley, Southampton ... Visits Upham, Durley and Curdridge.

Miss Martlew, 242, West Street, Fareham ... Health Visitor.

DISTRICT NURSES.

		Telephone.	
Nurse E. A. Townsend. West Hoe House, Bishop's Waltham, Southampton		Bishop's Waltham	174
,, A. L. Brown, 8, Shore Crescent, Bishop's Waltham. Southampton			
,, A. E. E. Polk, Black Horse Lane, Shirrell Heath, Southampton			
,, S. Reid, Nightingale Bungalow, Soberton, Southampton		Wickham	3182
,, D. E. Plowman, 31, West Street, Southwick, Fareham			
,, S. Cryer, Chase Cross Roads, Waltham Chase, Southampton		Bishop's Waltham	23
,, M. A. McHardy, Springfield Cottage, Westmeon, Petersfield			
,, N. A. Swain, High Street, Hambledon, Portsmouth			
,, W. Broomfield, Benares, Grange Road, Botley, Southampton			
,, D. L. Stoyell, " Leehurst," Botley, Southampton.			

PARISH WARDENS.

Bishop's Waltham	W. R. Gunner, Esq., " Ridgemede," Bishop's Waltham	Bishop's Waltham	28
Boarhunt	C. A. Vince, Esq., The Stores, Wickham Common	Wickham	2167
Corhampton and Meonstoke	F. A. Cooke, Esq., Post Office, Meonstoke	Droxford	63
Durley	W. Churcher, Esq., " Byways," Durley, Southampton	Durley	26
Curdridge	Colonel W. M. Coldstream, Oak Avenue, Curdridge	Bishop's Waltham	78
Denmead	F. Jesse, Esq., " The Shanty," Anmore Road, Denmead	Hambledon (P.O.)	72
Droxford	L. R. C. McIntosh, Esq., Post Office, Droxford	Droxford	66
Exton	G. W. Worthington, Esq., Post Office, Exton	Droxford	41

APPENDIX—Continued.

PARISH WARDENS—*(Continued)*.

Hambledon	Commander C. B. Roberts, Kennett Lodge, Hambledon	Hambledon 33
Shedfield	L. Hills, Esq., Shedfield, Southampton	Wickham 3170
Soberton	E. J. H. Matthews, Esq., Yew Tree Farm, Soberton	
Southwick	C. J. Willoughby, Esq., The Old Vicarage, Southwick	Cosham (Home).... 76586
		Cosham (Office) 75386
Swanmore	E. W. Jacobs, Esq., Chapel Road, Swanmore	
Upham	E. G. Gregg, Esq., Brushmakers' Arms, Upham	Durley.... 31
Preshaw	J. Oxer, Esq., Preshaw, Upham, Southampton	Bishop's Waltham 31
Warnford	R. G. Harris, Esq., Chestnut Cottage, Warnford	Westmeon 60
Westmeon	R. Russell, Esq., School House, Westmeon	
Wickham	H. R. Knight, Esq., " Glenmead," Wickham, Fareham	Wickham 3154

POLICE.

Fareham	Fareham 2285
Wickham	Wickham 2112
Bishop's Waltham	Bishop's Waltham 17
Droxford	Droxford 8
Soberton	Wickham 3181
Shedfield	Wickham 3120
Southwick	Cosham 76616
Hambledon	Hambledon 25
Portsmouth	Portsmouth 2011
Upham	Durley.... 34

REST CENTRES.

Telephone.

Bishop's Waltham	Rev. N. H. Stubbs, The Rectory, Bishop's Waltham, Southampton.	Bishop's Waltham	118	The Social Club, Houchin Street, Bishop's Waltham. Girls' and Infants' School, Bishop's Waltham. Boys' School, Bishop's Waltham Salvation Army Home, Station Road, Bishop's Waltham. Mission Hall, Ashton, Bishop's Waltham.
Boarhunt	Mr. H. Heath, Pound Farm, Boarhunt.			North Boarhunt Social Club, Boarhunt, Boar's Head Hall, Boarhunt.
Corhampton and Meonstoke	Rev. J. Stanning, The Rectory, Meonstoke, Southampton.	Droxford	99	Meon Hut, Meonstoke. Meonstoke School.
Curdridge	Colonel W. M. Coldstream, Oak Avenue, Curdridge, Southampton.	Bishop's Waltham	78	Reading Room, Curdridge. British Legion Club, Curdridge. Curdridge School.
Denmead	Mr. D. A. Cleary, School House, Denmead, Portsmouth.			Free Church School, Denmead. Denmead Council School. Collegiate School, Denmead. Denmead Church Hut.
Droxford	Mr. A. V. Carter, High Street, Droxford, Southampton.	Droxford	119	Council School, Droxford. Droxford Church Hall.
Durley	Mrs. R. M. Vaughan, Brook Cottage, Durley, Southampton.			Memorial Hall, Durley. Durley Council School.
Hambledon	Lady Taylor, " Whitedale," Hambledon, Portsmouth.	Hambledon	2	Hambledon Council School.
Shedfield	Mrs. Franklyn, New Place, Shedfield, Southampton.	Wickham	2121	Shedfield School and Reading Room. Methodist School, Shedfield. Chase Hut, Waltham Chase.
Soberton	Miss Lobb, Newtown School, Newtown, Fareham.			Soberton Council School, Newtown, Soberton.
Southwick	Mrs. Darlington, Oak Lodge, Southwick, Fareham.	Cosham	76669	Southwick Council School.
Swanmore	Mrs. Portal, " Holywell," Swanmore, Southampton.	Droxford	21	Swanmore Church School, Swanmore. Hall at Bricklayers' Arms, Swanmore. Swanmore Parish Hall. British Legion Club, Swanmore.
Upham	Mrs. E. Watson, The Rectory, Upham, Southampton.	Durley	36	Upham School. Upham Mission Hall.
Westmeon	Mrs. J. Jefferies, The Grange, Westmeon, Petersfield.	Westmeon	27	Westmeon Council School. Westmeon Territorial Drill Hall.
Wickham	Miss May, Wickham Lodge, Wickham, Fareham.	Wickham	3115	Wickham Junior Mixed School. Wickham Church Hall. Wickham Victory Hall.

SANATORIA.

Telephone.

Hants County Council Sanatorium	Chandler's Ford 2418
Sanatorium, The Mount, Bishopstoke, Eastleigh	Eastleigh 87235

APPENDIX—Continued.

WOMEN'S VOLUNTARY SERVICES.

Parish Representatives.

			Telephone.	
Bishop's Waltham	Mrs. Stubbs, The Rectory, Bishop's Waltham, Southampton		Bishop's Waltham	118
Boarhunt	Mrs. Mears, 8, Council Houses, North Boarhunt, Fareham			
Corhampton and Meonstoke	Mrs. Stanning, The Rectory, Meonstoke, Southampton		Droxford	99
Curdridge	Lady Colvin, Curdridge House, Curdridge, Southampton		Bishop's Waltham	40
Denmead	Miss F. Everitt, The Mill House, Denmead, Portsmouth			
Droxford	Mrs. Tudway, "Meonlea," Droxford, Southampton		Droxford	19
Durley	Miss Barton, Durley Lodge, Durley, Southampton		Durley	3
Hambledon	Mrs. Handcock, Folly House, Hambledon, Portsmouth		Hambledon	100
Shedfield	Mrs. Dreyer, Cam Cottages, Shedfield, Southampton		Wickham	2193
Soberton	Mrs. Warburton-Lee, Soberton Mill, Swanmore, Southampton		Wickham	3118
Southwick and Widley	Mrs. Darlington, Oak Lodge, Southwick, Fareham		Cosham	76669
Swanmore	Mrs. Sandell, Vicarage Lane, Swanmore, Southampton			
Upham	Mrs. Norton, Manor House, Upham, Southampton		Durley	29
Warnford	Mrs. Locke, Chestnut Cottage, Warnford, Southampton		Westmeon	60
Westmeon	Mrs. Baker-Cresswell, Home Paddocks, Westmeon, Petersfield		Westmeon	41
Wickham	Mrs. Bird, Park Place, Wickham, Fareham		Wickham	447

Clothing Depots.

	Stored at.	Clothing Officer.	Telephone.	
Bishop's Waltham	Northbrook House	Mrs. Paul, "Middlebrook," Bishop's Waltham	Bishop's Waltham	148
Boarhunt	Goathouse Farm, North Boarhunt	Miss Honess, North Boarhunt		
Corhampton, Meonstoke and Exton	Meonstoke Rectory	Mrs. Stanning, The Rectory, Meonstoke	Droxford	99
Curdridge	Curdridge Croft	Lady Somerville, Curdridge Croft, Curdridge	Botley	58
Denmead	"Greylands," Denmead	Miss Everitt, Mill House, Denmead		
Droxford	Manor House	Mrs. Tudway, Droxford	Droxford	19
Durley	Durley Lodge	Miss Barton, Durley Lodge, Durley	Durley	3
Hambledon	Fairfield House	Mrs. Handcock, Folly House, Hambledon	Hambledon	100
Shedfield	The Vicarage	Mrs. Hallifax, Red House, Shedfield	Wickham	3145
Soberton	c/o Miss Horwell, Newtown School	Mrs. Edwards, "Maypoles," Five Trees, Soberton	Droxford	124
Southwick	Oak Lodge	Mrs. Wesley, Flint Lodge, Southwick Park		
Swanmore	British Legion Hut	Mrs. Sandall, Upper Swanmore	Bishop's Waltham	195
Upham	Manor House	Mrs. E. Norton, Manor House, Upham	Durley	29
Warnford Westmeon	Home Paddocks	Mrs. Baker-Cresswell, Home Paddocks, Westmeon	Westmeon	41
Wickham	The Garage, Park Place	Mrs. Bird, Park Place, Wickham	Wickham	2139

MISCELLANEOUS ADDRESSES.

AMBULANCES.
Winchester Corporation. Winchester 536. Alton Isolation Hospital. Alton 2028.
Fareham Infectious Diseases Hospital. Fareham 2342.

HAMPSHIRE ASSOCIATION FOR CARE OF THE BLIND.
81, North Walls, Winchester. Tel.: Winchester 1503.

PORTSMOUTH SOCIAL SERVICE EMERGENCY COUNCIL.
Southern Secondary School, Portsmouth. Tel.: Portsmouth 31256.

Editors Footnote

The various deletions, and asterisks feature in the Original retained documentation.

Appendix: E

THE LATE
MRS. C. E. PORTAL

Old Swanmore Resident

The death of Mrs. Clara Ethel Portal, of Holywell House, Swanmore, came as a great shock to the village. Mrs. Portal passed away on Saturday, a few days after an accident in her home, at the age of 84 years. She will be greatly missed, as she always took a great interest in the activities of Swanmore, and was always willing to help.

Mrs. Portal was very fond of flowers and took a great interest in the British Legion Flower Show, as also in the British Legion Women's Section. being at one time Hon. Secretary. In spite of her age she collected regularly for Earl Haig's Poppy Fund.

The inquest was held at Winchester Guildhall on Monday afternoon, when the Winchester City Coroner (Mr. B. L. Bremridge) returned a verdict of accidental death.

The deceased's cook, Miss Lilly Williams, said that on the evening of June 9th Mrs. Portal went up to the bathroom, leaving her watching the T.V. Later she heard a bang and left the sitting room to find out what caused it. She found Mrs. Portal half-way down the stairs and suggested calling the doctor, but Mrs. Portal replied "Nonsense, I'll be alright."

The Coroner read a statement by Mrs. Portal in hospital, in which she said she went to the bathroom when it was still fairly early in the evening, and had her bath without putting the light on. However, by the time she was ready to leave the bathroom, it was quite dark, and in groping for the light switch she fell down the stairs.

Dr. Ronald Gibson, of Southgate-street, Winchester, said death was due to haemorrhage, resulting from fractured ribs.

Mrs C E Portal Obituary - Hampshire Chronicle 18Jun1960

Editors Footnote

As we have seen in the preceeding pages Mrs Portal played an extremely prominent role in the village during World War II both as Chairman of the Swanmore Invasion Committee and President of the Womens Institute.

139

Bibliography

Bates, H.E.   1945   Flying Bombs over England, Edited by Bob Ogley

Calder, Angus   1969   The People's War: Britain 1939-45, London,
                                  Jonathan Cape

Emery, Grace   1991   Some of the History of Shedfield Parish, Southampton,
                                  Paul Cave Publications

Evans, Pam   1999   Open University Degree Thesis (Introduction)

Harrison, Tom   1976   Living through the Blitz, New York, Schoken.

Stone, R.A.   1996   The Meon Valley Railway, Cheltenham,
                                  Runpast Publications

Langdon Davies, John 1941   Home Guard Warfare, Routledge

Lund and Ludlam   1971   Trawlers go to War, Foulsham

Watkins, Peter R   1995   A History of St Barnabas Church, Swanmore, 1845 1995,
                                  Published locally

Watkins, Peter R   2001   Swanmore since 1840, an illustrated history of a
                                  Hampshire village, Swanmore Books

About the Editor (and his team)

Keith Harrington

Born in Orpington, Kent	1936
WW2 evacuated to Somerset	1940-2
Educated at St Dunstan's College, Catford	1947-1953
Joined Nat Pro Bank, retiring as a Nat West Manager	1953-1990
Including a period on National Service with the RAF	1955-1957

Keith is now a Family Historian, operating his own business, Harringtons Heritage, having obtained a Certificate in English Local History from Portsmouth University. He is a Member of both the Association of Professional Genealogists and the Association of Genealogists and Researchers in Archives. Keith moved to 9 Glendale in 1975, with his wife Joan, daughters Dawn and Clare, and son Ian, who sadly died in 1998. He previously compiled the Swanmore Roll of Honour, published locally in 2002.

Gloria Atkinson-Carter

In 1975 Gloria Atkinson-Carter came to Swanmore with her husband, John, and two children, Blair and Nicola. She has worked at The University of Winchester (ex King Alfred's College and University College Winchester) for many years and retired as Senior Officer in 1999. She was asked to continue working at the University to edit a book on the College's Winton Lectures and since then has prepared copy for award-winning publications for the College. She now works in the Research & Knowledge Transfer Centre, helping prepare for the University's application for research degree-awarding powers.

Gloria is an active member of the St Barnabas Mothers' Union and is a founder member of the Swanmore Conservation Group.

Doug Braund

After gaining a degree in Mathematics at Clare College, Cambridge, Doug spent all his working life in the computer industry, including over 25 years based at IBM's Development Laboratory at Hursley, and then twelve years as a freelance technical author. With his wife Heather, he lived for nearly 32 years in Swanmore, where they brought up three children, but during the preparation of this book they retired to Worcestershire.

Photos (Back Cover)

Centre
The reverse of The Defence Medal
(for eligibility details see page 3).

Top Left
Swanmore Cub Camp 1939.

Top Right
District Guide Camp V. J. Day 1945
which includes Swanmore Guides.

Bottom
Tanks and Armoured Vehicles in the build up to D-day in one of the shady lanes between
Swanmore and Droxford.

Insert
Centre of front cover of Swamore Invasion Committee War Book.